S0-AIQ-085

Table of contents

CHAPTER 1: Girlfriend! The FROU

CHAPTER 2: Men and Women: Sharing Worlds, But from Distant Planets

CHAPTER 3: Hardly the Norm: Accidents and Sheer Wonders

CHAPTER 4: Food Fit for Foodies and Kitchen Capers

CHAPTER 5: Feelings, Oh, Oh, Oh, Feelings

Advance praise...

"Ann Ipock launched a signature collection of books that has wowed us ever since. She has successfully merged the amusing and the intellectual. Although her work includes quirky details, each book is as elegantly tailored as any fashion show outfit that made it down the runway."

—NANCY RHYNE, author of *Low Country Voices*

"Ann Ipock is a leading authority on the fabulous dynamics of FROU (Females Rule Our Universe). Zany and wise, she leads us from the wondrous world of FROU to 'Family Zoo and Pesky Relatives,' 'Accidents and Sheer Wonders' and much, much more. 'Life Is Short, So Read This Fast' and marvel!"

—ELIZABETH ROBERTSON HUNTSINGER WOLF, author of *Ghosts of Georgetown*

"*Life Is Short, So Read This Fast!* is a laugh-out-loud tribute to those things we Southern girls hold dear: good breeding, good friends, good food, and good gossip! Bless her heart, Ann Ipock celebrates our idiosyncrasies and paints them with pride."

—JAYNE JAUDON FERRER, author of *Dancing with My Daughter*

"From a touching meditation on the kitchen table to a long chuckle at Doctor Barbie Doll's expense, Ann celebrates daily life as if it's the parade she once enjoyed aboard the FROU float—and as if we should join her in waving."

—RANDALL A. WELLS, author of *Swamp, Strand, & Steamboat*

"Yo, readers! Ann Ipock's hilarious stories are just the ticket for a fast departure from the worries of the world. You'll find yourself grinning, identifying, and commiserating. The woman can tell a tale in the most delightful way. I'm a huge Ipock fan!"

—BETH BOSWELL JACKS, editor of usadeepsouth.com and author of *SNIPPETS I and II*

"*Life Is Short, So Read This Fast!* will have you nodding your head in agreement as you laugh out loud at what makes Southern Belles the charmers at parties and Steel Magnolias at managing their families and the community at large."

    —JOYCE DIXON, *Southern Scribe*

"Ann Ipock is Southern. And for us Southerners, we appreciate a good story. Ann is a gifted writer whose stories spark reaction, recall, and relaxation. Her humor is contagious, always putting a smile on your face and provoking laughter. You swear sometimes she's writing about your life experiences, and that's what makes Ann the best at what she does... writing, Southern style."

    —DWIGHT E. MCKENZIE, president and publisher of *Georgetown Times*

"Amazing! How does she keep coming up with these humorous anecdotes on the events of our daily lives? Ann Ipock is truly a talented, humorous writer that will entertain you and put a smile on your face."

    —DELORES BLOUNT, publisher of Strand Media Group, Inc.

"Once again, highly entertaining!"

    —GREG EVERETT, publisher of *Myrtle Beach Herald*

"Ann Ipock's talent for writing laugh-out-loud stories about family and everyday life is in a class by itself—a true Southern treasure. Quirky and real (you can't make this stuff up!), they're a colorful collage of humorous observations that make me wish she lived right next door."

    —KRISTY S. JOHNSON, publisher and editor-in-chief of *Columbia County Magazine*

"If it's deep fried and got sugar in it, it's genuinely Southern. So's Ann Ipock. Her observations and love of Southern life are charming, comforting and downright comical."

    —BETH POLSON, author and executive producer of TV movies including "The Christmas Box" and "Go Toward the Light"

"Ann's stories are always out of the box because Ann lives out of the box. You'll view life differently after reading [this]. She's Southernly sassy, and her sincerity and charm are outshined only by her wit!"

    —DIANE DEVAUGHN STOKES, TV host of "Southern Style"

GTS

Dear Ann,   9/11/07

Life Is Short,
So Read This Fast!

Happy reading
Ann Ipock

ANN IPOCK

Life Is Short, So Read This Fast! by Ann Ipock

GOODY 2 SHOES
PUBLISHING

published by
Goody 2 Shoes Publishing
PO Box 3212
Pawleys Island, SC 29585

First edition 2007.
Copyright ©2007 by Ann Ipock.

ISBN-10: 0-9676079-2-2
ISBN-13: 978-0-9676079-2-4

All rights reserved. Except for brief quotations embodied in critical articles and
reviews, no part of the contents of this book may be reproduced or transmitted
in any form or by any means without written permission of the publisher.

Portions of this book have appeared in different form in *Georgetown Times, Myrtle
Beach Herald, Sasee,* and *Pee Dee Magazine* and are reprinted with permission.

Applied for Library of Congress Cataloging-in-Publication Data

To contact the author for speaking engagements:
e-mail: amipock@sc.rr.com   *Web site:* www.annipock.com

Cover photograhy: Chuck Gee and K. Scott Whitaker;
BMW Z4 courtesy of Lavin Cars (Myrtle Beach, SC)

book design and production by Whitline Ink Incorporated
114 S. Carolina Ave., Boonville, NC 27011 *ph:* 336-367-6914
e-mail: info@whitlineink.com   *Web site:* www.whitlineink.com

13 12 11 10 09 08 07   7 6 5 4 3 2 1

Proudly printed in the United States of America.

CHAPTER 6: Let's Get Physical, or Perhaps Metaphysical

CHAPTER 7: Family Zoo and Pesky Relatives

CHAPTER 1
Girlfriend! The FROU

FROU:
Females Rule Our Universe
(But Don't Tell the Men)

Talk about fun! Recently, the FROUs and I rode on a float at the annual Fourth of July parade in my hometown, Pawleys Island, South Carolina, which also happens to be the oldest seaside resort in America. Around here, this parade happens to be *the* event of the year. Folks plan their vacations years in advance, renting seaside cottages or staying at their summer homes, in anticipation of the celebration. The morning of the parade, spectators gather at the edge of the road, sitting on lawnchairs or standing in the shade, as the parade entrants line up on the South Causeway. Anyone can enter and as they say, "the more the merrier."

Floats consist of pick-up trucks, boats on trailers, flatbed trucks, unicyclists, and anything else with wheels. Some entries have elaborate themes; others keep it simpler and smaller. There's a real mixture of people on the floats: children ride along with their parents; college friends gather from other parts of the state; families and friends who continue to celebrate all day; plus locals thrown in here and there. Trophies are awarded to the winners in several categories. Some folks really go all out. I know, because we did—the FROUs, that is.

Let me tell you about FROU, which stands for "Females Rule Our Universe." We are a group of wild and crazy women who, as the song goes, "just wanna have fun." In our close group of ten that day, we had the following: a book store owner, an editor, an administrative assistant, a publisher, a director of volunteers, two students, a retired businesswoman, a photography studio owner, and me. We were as diverse as the South itself: blondes, brunettes, and redheads; career women and those still in school; and one retiree. But we all have one thing in common: We embody the very qualities of the South that define us: charming, graceful, genteel, warm, mannered. And on top of that, we love holidays and celebrations! We are all about fun. (Plus, we love make-up, jewelry, hair care, and darling shoes.)

We decorated our float using colorful, hand-scripted signs and banners. One read, "Who are the FROUs? Doctors, artists, engineers, hairstylists, lawyers, teachers, preachers, etc." Another banner read, "What do FROUs do? Shop, dance, play, get mani's and pedi's, pray, read, volunteer, raise families, cook, garden, create, eat out…" Of course, we also displayed the American flag because we are a patriotic bunch. After all, this holiday was the celebration of our country's independence. Other banners read, "God bless America. God bless you. God bless FROU."

We were dressed in signature hot pink clothes, wigs and hats, over-done jewelry, and white gloves. Some of us wore frilly skirts— oh, we do love femininity! We carried parasols that we decorated individually, the object being who could fix up the most outlandish parasol. (It turned out we needed them in the sweltering heat.) We sang along to the music of Aretha Franklin, Shania Twain, Patti LaBelle, and we even threw in one by Roy Orbison. After all, we love womankind *and* mankind—and Roy was a great singer. We also threw out bags of what I call FROU candy, otherwise known as boiled peanuts, our Southern specialty. Russell, my hubby (whom I affectionately refer to as Oscar the Grouch), was our driver; but hard as I tried, I could not get him to wear pink, not even a pink bandanna on his Panama Jack straw hat.

The parade is over now and we are settled back into our regular, normal (if there is such a thing) lives. I'm kind of sad that it's over, but that's also a positive thing. Now we have a full year to brainstorm, plan, and create. Most of all, we want to say thank you to the absolutely huge crowd that spurred us on, giving us sweet smiles, throwing lip-smacking kisses, and even tossing us Hershey's Kisses!

Test Your FROU IQ

Ever since our FROU float rode in the Pawleys Island Fourth of July parade, folks have been asking, "What exactly is a FROU?" Although I explained it before as merely "Females Rule Our Universe," I'll give you some solid examples to determine if you might be a FROU.

YOU MIGHT BE A FROU IF:

+ It takes you longer to remove your jewelry than it does to remove your clothes.

+ You wrap gifts in fur, feathers, or suede.

+ You call folks dahlin', sweetie, angel, or sugah and mean it.

+ Your manicure appointment takes precedent over a root canal.

+ You refuse to drink a beverage (probably sweet tea with lemon) without a straw.

+ You keep five various shades of lipstick in your purse at all times.

+ You pack matching purses for your shoes when traveling.

+ You wear pink or you wear red, but never both at the same time.

+ You avoid dishwashing, gardening, and cleaning without wearing gloves.

+ You decorated at least one room in your home entirely in pink.

+ Your nickname is Flossie, Prissy, or anything ending with Lou.

+ You ride in at least one holiday parade per year.

+ You put up a string of decorative lights anytime of year, anywhere in your house.

+ You can chew gum and file your nails at the same time.

+ You refer to lunch with your girlfriends as "lunchie."

- You borrow your teenager's clothes, or she borrows yours.
- Your musical taste includes Etta James, Barry White, James Taylor, and Sting.
- Your grandchildren call you Gigi, Mimi, Chi-Chi, or Ree-Ree.
- Your favorite season is a full moon.
- You say hello and goodbye with a kiss on the cheek.
- Your perfume is so rare you can only order it online.
- You enter a room and everyone stops talking.
- You can't see your refrigerator door for party invitations.
- You give away a smile each day, or give an anonymous gift.
- You end every day with a hot, relaxing bubble bath.
- You read this list and smile.

Being in a Woman's Fun Club—I Can Dig It!

There's never been a better time in history to be a woman than right now. Do you realize that the female gender has so many choices for camaraderie that it's almost a shame *not* to get involved in a "fun club" (not a "fan club" but a "fun club"). Hence, fun!

The choices are endless: Ya Ya Sisterhood, Sweet Potato Queens, and the Red Hat Society (whose enormous membership, by the way, could easily form a third major political party in this country).

My friend and author Ronda Rich writes about her group, the Dixie Divas. I, myself, am a member of the FROUs. The main objective of these clubs is frivolous fun! Never before have we girl-friends had such choices. While it's true that we've held member-ships in other clubs for years—Junior League, Rotary Club, and Pilot Club, to name a few—these clubs have strict rules: You must attend meetings, pay fees, and join committees. Admittedly, they do great things—fostering good will, boosting the economy, and rais-ing money for worthwhile causes. Lots of hard work, but where's the pure, effortless fun?

Other clubs provide activity and entertainment. In this group, members have something in common and they interact with one another: Bunko, bridge, Mahjong, or book club. Great idea, but you have to think so hard—not to mention the stress. Again, where's the fun? Here's a little secret: Sometimes fun club members actually use the club façade as an excuse to merely socialize or to just get out of the house, but don't tell the husbands who are home, cooking, help-ing kids with homework, and doing laundry.

I remember my mother was in a group called The Sewing Club, yet no one ever sewed a stitch at a meeting. Shoot! The words "mate-rial," "pattern," "needle" or "thread" were never spoken—I'm not even sure they held meetings, now that I think about it. It was more or less a social thing. However, and this is very important, the group hosted a formal dance once a year—a real swanky affair—"The Sewing Club Dance." There was a waiting list to get in the "club" just to attend the annual soiree.

The ladies' "fun clubs" I mentioned have no requirements: no working, thinking, or competing. Their goal is just uber enjoyment. Oh, and if you don't know which club to join, no problem, just start your own. Find about a half dozen friends who want to get together occasionally to chill out. Have a meeting, give yourself some snappy name, and next thing you know, everyone wants to join. Your membership will swell when news gets around town because it's in our female genes to be nosy and nervy. Drop your club's name at a gathering of any kind and conversation will stop dead in its tracks. Watch some gossipy woman whisper to her best friend, "Did you hear Mary Lou talking about the 'Fourth Tuesday Come-As-You-Are-Club?' Why, I've never heard of it! How do you get invited? Who goes? Where do they meet?" There. Now, do you see now why it's never been a better time to be a woman?

Men, on the other hand, would flat-out reject the idea of a "fun club." Is that because they're often stick-in-the-muds? Or is it because they are just not programmed to hang out and chit-chat? (Russell, my hubby, says it's the programming answer.) Men prefer poker clubs, tennis or golf groups, hunting clubs, and more serious clubs. No wonder men don't have "fun clubs." What would they talk about? Sports? The stock market? Their jobs? They'd never discuss anything as personal as a hernia operation, a crazy twin brother living in Atlanta, or hair transplants. We women proudly blab about that. And we should! So we do. And we will continue!

I've never been one to follow rules, so the clubs with rules don't appeal to me. This is not bragging, it's just honest. In fact, this rebelliousness got me into a whole heap of trouble in sixth grade when Mrs. Jackson, my near-ninety-year-old teacher with dragon breath, a white hair bun (in a *net*, no less!) and size ten black granny boots, screamed, "No one, absolutely no one, is allowed to wear their shirt tails out. I've heard of some hooligans down the hall pushing their luck, but I won't tolerate it in my classroom!" Her huge lumbering body seemed nine feet tall to me and she had a booming voice that could echo across the Grand Canyon. I was definitely afraid of her, and yet, the temptation was too great. Her order seemed more like a dare to me and my friend Jane. We went into the bathroom during lunch, pulled our shirt tails all the way out, and watched our teacher's horror-stricken face as we strolled back into the classroom and sat down.

We thought we were being funny. She obviously did not. Staying after school and writing, "I will listen to Mrs. Jackson in the future and not take out my shirt tail" a hundred times pretty much cured us. Even now, many years later, with the current style being to wear shirt tails out, I still feel uncomfortable doing so.

And finally, "fun clubs" make us feel like we belong, like we're special. I think it's just human nature to want to belong—and that's a good thing. To belong in a certain group, be it family or friends; to feel accepted, loved, and wanted. At the very core of the human race, these are the primary basic yearnings. That, and the once-in-a-lifetime chance to appear on *Oprah*—yeah, like that will ever happen! (Well, maybe.) But being in a "fun club" with no rules? Ahhhhh, now that sounds perfect. Kind of like the Outback Steakhouse jingle, "No rules, just right!" I can dig it.

Ready for a New You?
Try a Wig

Little did I realize how a new hairstyle could change your life. It can certainly change how you feel about yourself, and in some cases, can even change your personality. And when I refer to the word "hairstyle," I don't mean a shampoo and cut, color, perm, or straightener. I am talking about a new hairstyle (and a new you) via a beguiling, bewitching, bodacious wig.

All this new knowledge began at a local café when I recently met Glenda, owner of The Wig Shop. We just seemed to click. I was intrigued with her friendliness and vivacious spirit. I especially admired her beautiful coif—soft golden hair with a delicate wave and absolutely no split ends. When we said goodbye, I told Glenda I'd come by her shop soon.

Meeting Glenda that day made me think seriously about the art of wig-wearing. The only experience I've ever had wearing a wig was in community theatre. Wigs weren't exactly the rage then.

But now things have changed. I learned this the day I visited The Wig Shop and talked with Cindy (Glenda was out), who is a master at her craft. We chatted like old friends, sharing stories and laughing at similar, unpredictable lives. Before I could say "bleached blonde," she had me modeling at the mirror: long wigs, short wigs, blonde and red wigs, some with hair bands, some with large combs, some extensions, some additions, and some full wigs. It was uproariously fun! Each wig was so super silky I felt like Rapunzel. These wigs have no frayed ends, no stray fuzzy pieces, and no gray strands poking through the blonde highlights (like my own hair). They are perfect! Did I mention that they are also very natural looking? I promise you can't spot who does and who doesn't wear one anymore. Instead of, "Only her hairdresser knows for sure," the term has become, "Only her wigmaker knows for sure."

And another thing: Wigs are empowering! The transformation

is incredible. One minute you feel like a Daring Diva; the next, a showgirl in Las Vegas. You can feel your demeanor change as you channel Jennifer Aniston, Goldie Hawn, or Raquel Welch with just the flip of a wig. In fact, I was flitting all over that store, wishing I had a feather boa draped around my neck, or perhaps a pair of stiletto heels and fishnet stockings, to complete my new ensemble. The vast array of choices is staggering and the prices are honestly quite fair. Funny thing is, for the cost of about a two-hour hair appointment for "the works" at a salon, you can buy a wig. But don't get carried away, it's not as simple as you think. Sure, it's easy to reason it all out, saying, "I could save X number of dollars by not going to the beauty shop and buy a wig instead." (That's exactly how my left-brained husband, Russell, reasons things out.) Wrong! It simply doesn't work that way because your own hair still needs attention in the form of the usual cut, color (maybe), and style.

The day I visited, Cindy and I finally narrowed down my choice to a short bob. It looked identical to my present hair, but with so much more body. This thing bounced like a baby on a trampoline, and emitted a shine that was nearly blinding. With Cindy's urging, I stood there, doing quarter-turns in the mirror like a beauty pageant contestant, admiring the sides and back. Each profile looked better than the last one.

Finally I said, "I want it!" Cindy said, "Then you should get it." But my head hurt (literally) from thinking through all the choices and I decided to go home and sleep on it (my head, not the wig). Before I left, I tried on my favorite for a final time. When I removed it, omigosh, what a let down. What I saw was disgusting: my own flat, limp, dull, hair. Heck, I bet no one ever leaves the shop *not* purchasing a wig because they'd look like Phyllis Diller (who really did need a wig, by the way). I didn't want to pick the wrong one, so I told her I'd return in a week or two. Then I looked around for a bag. Cindy asked why I wanted a bag. "To cover up my head, or should I say, my hair? I can't go out in public looking like this!" Then I searched for some scissors to cut two holes in the bag for my eyes.

Here's to beauty, brains, and big-wig hair! And I promise when I don my new 'do, everyone will be asking, "Did she or didn't she?"

High Maintenance: Is This You?

In these politically correct times, I realize it might not be kosher to make fun of the opposite sex—in this case, your spouse. But a list of relationship-killers does come to mind. You know, those annoying people that get under your skin, grate on your nerves, and make you run for cover. We've all known them. Heck, some of us have *been* them. In fairness, I admit Russell *is* easier to get along with than I am. But please don't tell him I said so. It would give him an unfair advantage to any upcoming arguments we might have.

Russell defines me as, well, in a word or two, *high maintenance*. "Nuh uh," is my response, as I quite maturely defend myself with a sneer, then drop my jaw and stick out my chin *just so*. Can I help it if I'm picky, opinionated, and sometimes demanding? That is *not* necessarily the same thing as high maintenance. I remind Russell that if it weren't for my little quirks, he might not have ended up as my husband. That's when his eyes light up as if there's a flashlight shining behind them. Like he could be thinking, *Maybe there's still hope, maybe she'll change her mind*. It's kind of scary, really.

One day as we were bantering over what is high maintenance versus an out-right "pain in the drain," I asked him to give me some examples of what he meant by being HM, as I dubbed it, and this is what he said. (Keep in mind these are not necessarily things that only I've done, but rather a few family members that span a generation or two. Don't ask me who though 'cause I'm not naming names!)

YOU MIGHT BE HIGH MAINTENANCE IF:

1. You ask your husband to help pull up your pantyhose because your nails aren't dry, and could he speed it up or else you'll be late!

2. You request your waiter bring you eight different sauces on eight different occasions in the span of thirty minutes, while a throng of hungry diners stand nearby waiting for a table.

3. You go to the Saks Fifth Avenue customer service desk and tell them you'd like one of their fancy, embossed boxes with the silky tissue paper. Then you go home and deposit in it Aunt Gertrude's present that you bought at the Dollar Store.

4. You ask your husband to stop mowing the lawn long enough to come in and vacuum the floor after he sweeps the kitchen and cleans the bathrooms, telling him you're off to a twelve-hour sale.

5. You call your husband on his cellphone, interrupting his meeting with the boss—where he's pleading for a raise—to ask him if he's seen your library card.

6. You tell your 6' 2" "Big & Tall" husband you two will have to sleep in the bedroom with the twin beds, lumpy mattresses and all, because your parents are coming to stay a few days and they need your queen-sized bed. Oh, and that your dad wants to borrow your hubby's C-PAP (breathing machine) to see if it really does control snoring.

7. You ask your exhausted shag-dance instructor, who just taught three back-to-back dance classes and is sweating like a pig, to spend an extra hour with you and your husband after class because you think y'all need clarification of the belly-roll.

8. You drive around looking for a *full-service* gas station until you nearly run out of gas because it's twenty-seven degrees outside and dang it, that fake mohair coat you bought at that 75%-off season-end sale sure won't keep you warm if *you* have to pump.

9. You beg your husband to climb out your bedroom window at two in the morning to kill a chirping cricket, saying, "You can't expect me to get any beauty rest with *that* going on, can you?"

10. Finally, you announce to your family that you're no longer cooking, citing that you're not appreciated, you're going on strike, and they'll just have to figure out their own meals. (Here's the heartbreak: Your husband says, "I didn't know you could cook!")

And though I wouldn't label Russell as HM *exactly*, he does have a few traits that I might identify as "bothersome." His laid back, lackadaisical, Forrest Gump-attitude I often chide him about is more like "low maintenance." So here's my criteria for LM:

<u>YOU MIGHT BE LOW MAINTENANCE IF</u>:

1. You walk out of any and every room in the house and leave the light on.

2. You gladly stay up until the wee hours of the morning to watch Duke basketball or the Masters golf tournament, but become unbelievably tired at the mere mention of a late-night dinner and dancing.

3. You promise to give your wife a foot rub, but fall asleep before she's even out of the shower.

4. You forget your wife's birthday, or worse, your anniversary.

5. You tell your wife you can't wash her car because quite frankly, you've never even washed your own car.

6. You chew ice or hard candy loudly near your wife's ear.

7. You alternately snore, then yank off all your wife's covers while doing what I call the "walrus roll," just as she is entering deep REM sleep.

8. You get lost while driving out of town—and continue on for two full hours with your wife napping beside you—because you're too stubborn to stop and ask for directions.

9. You bite your fingernails down to the quick when driving your wife's car, then she finds those horrid little slivers all over the floorboard.

10. You open a bag of potato chips, eat half of them, then throw the crumpled package back in the cabinet without a chip-clip.

Well, that's the big ten. Ten for HM and ten for LM. Do you see yourself, your spouse, or your significant other in any of these scenarios? Don't worry, it's all in fun. Nobody's perfect, and all this zaniness sure beats the heck out of dull, boring, and predictable. And, I ought to know, since I'm anything but!

Gotta Have Some Two-Ply TP and Paper Towels in the Bathroom or Else!

I'm taking a poll. How many people out there readily replenish the toilet paper holder when it's empty? Though it's especially annoying to run out of paper and find none in sight, it's also exasperating to find a roll but it's not in the dispenser. This is a pet peeve of mine. I mean, how tough can it be to push back that little spring, slide the new roll onto the silver cylinder, then pop it back in place? Done!

Russell's pet peeve is what he calls "John Wayne [a.k.a. "rough and tough"]" toilet paper—that cheap, itchy, cardboard-like *single ply* stuff. In fact, that is one splurge the man will whip out his wallet for, pronto. I fell victim (but only once) to an advertising ploy at a neighborhood drugstore that runs a TP sale every so often. They boast of a dozen rolls for some unheard of price, like $3.99. The packaging is colorful, eye-catching, and inviting—it's even a name brand! But when I bought it that one time, Russell complained for a month. Not really, it only took about a week for the two of us to use all twelve rolls! I think we subconsciously wanted it gone, so we used more than double what we needed. Then, one weekend when our daughter Katie was home from college, she accidentally fell victim to the same tissue purchase. That night, Russell came out of the bathroom moaning, "John Wayne." Katie thought he had lost his mind...but actually, I think he'd lost some skin!

When I told this story to my friend Belinda over lunch in an upscale restaurant the other day, she brought up some of her own bathroom pet peeves: First, she hates it when there is no paper towel dispenser in a public bathroom. (Me too.) And the wall-mounted hand-dryer "only makes matters worse, what, with the germy knob," she said. If this happens (and I think it's in defiance), Belinda told me she dries her hands with the normally-found one-ply TP, but this makes a mess—sticking to the inside of her fingers, leaving a tenacious spider web. Upon further discussion, I also discovered that she shares a strange habit. One that, until now, I only knew one other person in America had (our daughter, Katie). When she "finishes up" Belinda *steps* on the toilet handle with her shoe, instead of using her hand, to flush. Oh, that makes me sick because I'm the fool who uses the toilet after her and discovers grit, sand, and grime—not to mention germs on my hands. Argghhh! But after she steps on the handle (I asked her if she'd ever fallen down in the middle of her "karate chop," and she said no), she then washes her hands and dries them with a towel (or TP, like I said, if no towel is there).

This next part is more of a two-fold dilemma than a pet peeve: At this point, Belinda doesn't want to touch the dirty doorknob, so using her hands, she wraps the doorknob with the paper, then opens it. She then throws the paper in the trashcan, provided it's not on the other side of the room. If it is on the other side, she throws it and just hopes for the best. If it doesn't land inside the can, "too bad." She says she's not about to pick it up off the floor, because that would cancel out the entire hand-washing routine, and she'd have to start over. Now I know who is throwing those towels on the floor, and I'm appalled! In fact, that very day, I went to the bathroom after her and guess what I spotted on the floor? Girrrrll!

It's no wonder women's public toilets wear out twice as fast as men's. Belinda told me this and she's somewhat of an authority on the subject. She says it's because of the kicks and karate chops that women's toilets endure. She could not cite the source of this very important fact (I reminded her that she is contributing to the problem), but she did say she read it once while sitting on the toilet at home, and suddenly her phone rang. Jumping to attention because she was expecting an important call, she hobbled over about ten feet and answered. However, a big faux pas occurred: Not recognizing the caller and without thinking she said, "Can you hold on while I wipe, I mean, while I *write* your name down?" She returned to the bathroom, flushed, washed, and dried. But when she returned to the phone, no one was there. I'll bet it was a telemarketer—probably trying to sell a few cases of that single-ply toilet paper!

Hair Doo-zies:
The Bubble or the Stubble?

Sherrian, my hairdresser, is a saint. How do I know that? She has seen me through the roughest of times (okay, so, maybe it's more like *I created rough times for her*—sorry!) and she has seen me through the best of times (my "best" is simply not being so wishy-washy, and I promise I'm trying to change.) She never complains though, never grimaces (that I can see), never utters a cuss word. It's a miracle.

I started seeing Sherrian about three years ago when a friend recommended her to me. "You'll love it there!" she exclaimed. "It's just like 'Steel Magnolias,' only better." Having played the part of Truvy in that very play in the Murrells Inlet Community Theatre production, I was a little skeptical. After all, Truvy's beauty shop would be the ultimate hair salon. It was chock-full of all the enticements of life: juicy gossip, girlfriend heart-to-heart talks, helpful advice, remedies for healing. Add to that, beauty dished out professionally. My friend was right. Inlet Hair Design is all that and more.

Sherrian has "colored my world" with strawberry-blonde, then ash-blonde, then light-brunette, and back. She's trimmed my ends by way of razor-cut, then long layers, then no layers, then back to my current razor-cut.

Sherrian knows that what I really want is impossible, though she'd never actually tell me this. She cannot make me look like a combination of Meg Ryan, Charlize Theron, and Jane Krakowski all rolled into one. Goodness knows, she's tried. She and I both know a new hairdo won't do that, but she always gives it her best shot. When I describe the umpteenth different request for that visit—my bangs a little shorter, the top a little fuller, or the sides a little wispier—she smiles and says "Uh huh," or "I see." Then I really confuse her and say, "You know, the stubble-look. Get it?" Aren't I lucky that Sherrian is a mind-reader in addition to all her other talents?

I recently discovered a pillow on a sofa in their shop that states,

"A good hairstylist is a sheer delight!" The pillow was a gift to Beverly, another hair designer. Then there's Connie, who so kindly offered me the use of a wig for another play I was in two years ago.

Oh, and I saved the best part for last: Christmas! Honey, their Christmas holiday is unreal. The whole week of Christmas they receive cookies, candy, cake, and the bubbly stuff from their grateful clients. If you planned ahead during that week, you could eat lunch out with your girlfriends, stop by the shop for a quick, refreshing shampoo and style from one of the hands-free (i.e., non-snacking) stylists, and then enjoy dessert right on the spot.

Recently, Sherrian and I were discussing our wonderful husbands and how amazing they are to put up with us. For instance, I found out I'm not the only one who sleeps with a pillow, that runs lengthwise on the bed, marking "his" and "her" sides at our halfway point—75% for wives and 25% for husbands. We really do this to help support our back when we get in the sideways position, laying one knee over the supporting pillow. But it looks like we are staking out our territory. In fact, we both dare our husbands to cross over that well-defined line; though if we decide to cross over, that's okay. I mean, surely you know that rules often change when we're the ones making them. That's a plus of being a woman.

We have a lot in common. Sherrian and I both have children (actually, young adults) going to the University of South Carolina, and they're both members of the marching band. Our husbands look alike—same stature, build, and coloring. We both love cute jewelry and stylish shoes. Actually, I think all of the ladies who work there are the best of the bunch. I've witnessed handicapped clients come inside and one of the stylists always jump to open the door and escort the client to the chair. This warm welcome usually includes a hug. And this show of affection works both ways: I've seen clients bring them fresh vegetables out of their garden, house plants, flower bouquets—even kittens!

Most services provided there are pleasant, even relaxing. Shampooing for instance. I want to tell Sherrian to never, ever stop. Keep rubbing, *ahhhhhhhhh*, the scalp rub. But I know she must stop. There are other clients to be seen and the water bill to pay. However, other treatments are torture. Mustache-waxing, for instance. I find it odd that in mid-life, some men lose hair on their head...only for some women to discover hair on their upper lip. Another reason I love to go there is this place is so cool. I mean really cool, as in temperature. It's the only enclosed building in America where I don't have hot flashes. You'll never hear me say to Sherrian, "Is it just me, or is it hot in here?" like I do in lots of other shops.

I told Sherrian that on a recent trip to my parents' home in North Carolina, I noticed all the ladies at the country club were wearing their hair in the "bubble" style. Except for the color variations, they all looked alike. You had your blonde bubble, your red bubble, and your brunette bubble. I became worried. I wanted to make sure my current bed-head hairdo (the easiest 'do I've ever known) is not going out of style. "No honey," Sherrian reassured me, patting me on my shoulder.

Then we both decided this: Any hairdo that looks better first thing in the morning, even before brushing (messy is dressy!), looks even better with maximum-sustained winds while walking around the block (natural blow-dry), and is actually sort of cute when sweating at the gym (looks moussed when not-moussed) is the way to go. They can keep their bubble, but I'll take my stubble. And if Sherrian, the saint, said it, I know it's true.

A Hip-Hop Flip-Flop
for This Shoe-Crazy Ipock

What do flip-flop, hip-hop, and Ipock have in common? For starters, they all rhyme. Even more important, I can't believe flip-flops are so totally hip-hop. Fashionable, trendy, cool, and in style. And I can't believe that I, Ann Ipock, wear them everywhere.

There was a time when a woman wouldn't have been caught dead wearing flip-flops in public. I said the same thing years ago about rollers/curlers in women's hair, but I've never swayed on that thought. Flip-flops have been a different story. Now they're the rage. Young and old, teeny-boppers and grandmothers are sporting them. I've joined the masses to *expose my toes*, and not only my red-polished toes, but also my silver toe ring and silver anklet.

With Old Navy, Stein Mart, and Kohl's, I am styling. Not only styling, but I'm saving. For what money I've spent on flip-flops this summer, I would've spent triple that for regular shoes. Plus, you don't have to polish them, have them re-soled, or worry about scuff marks. They're practically maintenance-free.

Now, I've always been nicknamed the shoe queen by my friends, something to do with my vast and sordid collection. After all, I was born with a silver slipper on my foot, as opposed to a silver spoon in my mouth, since my father owned shoe stores. And that slipper just happened to be Stride Rite, low-top, white leather, with a thumb's growing width at the toes. I'm sure my parents had a pair on me before I could walk, and for sure, long before I could say "shooz."

In fact, my siblings and I went to work at the Bootery as a family custom, at age 14. Every Friday when Dad gave out paychecks, I returned about half of mine in order to pay for the shoes I was holding, which I had picked out the week before. I wish I had a dollar for every pair of Bass Weejuns I owned. My two sisters and brother did the same thing. Cathy, Nancy, Steve, and I were the best walking advertisement (pardon the pun) that the Bootery ever knew!

But, like I said, it hasn't been too terribly many years ago that I didn't leave the house without pantyhose and freshly-shined leather heels. Then along came sling-backs and they took over. Eventually sandals filled the spot. And now, at least for summer and here at the beach, it's flip-flops. And many pairs can be had for under $10.

You've got choice after choice. Rubber, leather, fabric, braided, raffia, linen. You've got wedges, platforms, flats. Every color you could ever want. Sometimes I end up with two pairs to match the same outfit. They're so affordable! Some have flowers, beads, confetti, stripes, or straw. But now that I own a dozen or so pairs, would somebody please tell me how to store them? I'm kind of a neat freak with my closet and these suckers don't come with a box. And you sure can't stack them. I searched for the right "shoe bag" and discovered the bag would cost more than all the flip-flops combined.

With all this positive exhilaration for flip-flops, I must be honest. There is one slight problem. How in the heck do you try them on in the store when they are always tied together with that little bitty plastic thingy that is strong enough to lift a car? And you have to try them on, because let's be frank, these things made in China are usually not sized like regular American shoes. I might wear a six and I might wear a nine. You place your left foot in one and your right foot in one and you try to take a step, and ha! The jerk of the secured plastic makes two shoes move and feel like one. Your feet are strangled as you can only walk four inches at a time, *swish-swash, swish-swash.* This is when you secretly pray no one is watching, but wonder if half the store is. Probably the employees are watching you on the hidden camera, having a laugh at your expense, cracking up at your jerky, creeping, unsteady travel.

And speaking of travel, we're going on a cruise to St. Marten, St. Thomas, and the Bahamas in October. I just hope all these flip-flops hold out until then, since the weather will be cold in October and the stores here will have in winter-wear selections. Choices then will include boots, lace-ups, and heels. I just can't see any of those matching my bathing suit, a fashion faux pas if I've ever seen one (a "rig" is what we Ipocks call it). And another problem is, then who could admire my sweet little silver toe ring?

Capris with Side Zippers Pose a Dangerous Trap

Side zippers are just one more irritating example of the puzzling complexities found in women's fashion today. They rank right up there with dresses that criss-cross in the back (or is it in the front—and does it criss-cross, or tie in a bow?), pointy-toed shoes that cause corns, and square buttons that won't stay buttoned.

Capri pants, in and of themselves, are great. They're popular and easy to find, maintaining a strong fashion hold for several years now. They're trouble-free, no alterations needed, since the hem is never a problem. But capris are notorious for having side—no, make that snide—zippers.

I've noticed a pattern lately. Most capris these days come with those annoying side zippers instead of front zippers. I don't understand why. It doesn't change the appearance one bit and they're a menace. First off, I can't *see* the zipper. Sure, I swivel my head down-and-left as far as possible, but a certain body part (I won't say what) obstructs my view. If I do succeed at zipping them, I end up pulling a muscle in my neck. Either way, the zipper often breaks, meaning it pulls away from the material. I'd like to think it's not my gaining weight, since this happens over and over. Sometimes the teeth/track of the zipper get stripped-out. Other times the zipper goes halfway up or down, and then gets stuck. I once read that rubbing a candlestick over the zipper will fix the problem. Ha! Don't fall for this, Women of America. My alteration lady asked me when replacing a zipper why the material was so slick, then laughed hysterically when I told her the reason.

When the side zipper does get stuck, and believe me, it will, it's always at the most inopportune time and inconvenient place. Believe me, I know. Recently, before exiting a bathroom inside a department store, I could only get the zipper halfway up. After scraping my fingers raw, my only option was to pull down on my cropped top and hold it flat, thus covering the gap. Even worse was when I went into the bathroom at the movie theatre last week and the zipper would not budge; and I really had to GO! Inside the stall, I could not wriggle out of those capris. I'm sure the lady waiting her turn wanted an explanation when she heard the commotion and saw my feet under the door, dancing a jig. Luckily, my adrenaline kicked in (the Fight or Flight Syndrome, I guess). Suddenly I became Super Zipper Woman. In one desperate twist, I jumped out of those suckers.

Maybe capris aren't so great after all when you consider the notorious side zipper. Even when I find them for $20 on sale, I'll end up spending half the original price on a new zipper. Does this make sense? No, not hardly. It's not fair!

Men, on the other hand, don't have to worry about side zippers. (Wouldn't that be a scream?) Come to think of it, plenty of fashion comparisons between men and women aren't fair. How about us women having to strip down inside those stuffy fitting rooms with putrid lights that cast green shadows while trying on clothes? Bathing suits try-ons are the most painful and tormenting clothes occasions of all.

Once again, men have it so good. They stroll into the store, pick out one of three sizes (small, medium, or large) and out they march with a Tommy Bahama swimsuit. Men's slacks are also purchased off the rack by simply grabbing their size—38/32, for instance. Very little work or thinking is required. (However, I can't really complain here because I prefer not to know my waist size.) Same easy process with men's shirts: 17-34/35, pick-up, pay the clerk, leave.

I wonder at what point clothing manufacturers said, "Let's make buying clothes easy on the men by using a simple numerical system. But for the women, hmmmm, let's give them a little more challenge. We'll start out with bras. Let's run them in sizes thirty-two to forty-two, which, granted is a broad range; but we'll offer even more choices with cup size. How about A to DD? And if that doesn't drive them crazy, we'll add panties in several sizes from four to twelve and up. According to the material and the style, on any given day, they'll be able to wear any, all, or none of these sizes."

But wait, y'all! It gets worse. "Now, just to throw in a little more confusion, we'll label blouses, slacks, skirts, shorts, and suits in even-numbered sizes to designate women's fashion. We'll use odd-numbered sizes for junior fashion." At this point, the Head Designer of the Fashion Board (probably a man) interrupted, "For heaven's sake! Women can handle more than that. They are built to triumph over adversity: cheating husbands, surly children, a household to run, hurricanes, tornadoes, and fires…so let's test them with side zippers." Argh!

Somewhere, right now, there is probably a prissy but storming-mad "It Girl," wearing Juicy Couture low-rise capris, swinging her Louis Vuitton handbag with one hand, and pulling her hair out with the other. Her side zipper is stuck and she can't leave the bathroom to rejoin her surprisingly gorgeous but clueless blind date. He's waiting at the table in a posh restaurant in a tony East Coast city. Eventually he'll notice she's gone and check on her. Let's hope at that point, someone hollers, "Is there a seamstress in the house?" She'll need one to get out of the mess she's in!

"How Do You Like Me Now?" on the Cover of *GS Magazine*

Like most kids, I often dreamed about what I wanted to be when I grew up: a movie star, model, or singer. In fact, in those days, my sisters and I did some modeling at the Bootery, our family shoe store. I never could sing, but I tried real hard. And I "acted" a little in the fourth grade when I pantomimed "Alley Oop" for our school talent show. But being an author of humor columns and three books has surpassed all of my childhood dreams.

And in a roundabout way, I really did become a model. Or, at least, I became a cover girl. When my publisher, Carolina Avenue Press, sent out media kits for my second book, *Life Is Short, But It's Wide*, to several nearby states, I immediately got calls for interviews, book signings, and general inquiries. But who would have guessed a magazine would not only want to interview me and review my book, but also place my photo on their cover?

How this scenario shaped up is a story in and of itself. Sara, the editor of *GS Magazine*, set up our interview at Barnes & Noble Café, where we chatted like old friends. She even admitted in the published write-up that at times it was hard to distinguish who was the interviewer and who was the interviewee.

Well, you must remember that I'm a freelance writer in many genres, and I have conducted interviews myself. Two outstanding women leap to mind: for *Gateway* magazine, Dorothea "Dottie" Benton Frank, *New York Times* best-selling author of three novels, the most recent being *Pawleys Island*; and for *Sasee* magazine, Robin Lee Simmons, founder and president of BooStudio Handbags, a nationally distributed product. And besides that, I'm just plain old nosey. When Sara asked about my children, I asked about hers. When she wanted to know where I went to school, I wanted to know where she went to school. It was like a ping-pong match: your turn, now my turn. What fun!

Next she sent Joe Carr, photographer extraordinaire, to my home for a photo shoot. That was a blast! Amanda Yerkes, a GS intern and Sara's assistant, also came. What a small world—I met Amanda recently at Collector's Café, where she is a part-time waitress. Somehow the subject came up that she's a nearby college student and an intern at GS Magazine. That's when I told her about the upcoming photo shoot and she knew all about it, saying she'd be there. The three of them marched into my home that day—Joe, Sara, and Amanda—armed with lights, cameras, and action. First came the staging. We moved the sofa forward, added lush green plants, and fluffed up the pillows. It seemed to me that photography is a little like Chinese cooking; both require precise, meticulous, arduous preparation, and then the actual work is a snap.

Early on I realized I'd forgotten to paint my fingernails red, which is my trademark. I asked if we could take a little break, though the job hadn't even begun. Joe said that wasn't a problem because he had lots of preparation to do (talk about a patient person). When I returned, upon his command I then sat down on my red sofa. (Something told me that was a great purchase when I selected the couch a year ago, though I'd never decorated with red before. And I certainly never guessed at the time I'd be posing for the Christmas issue of a popular magazine. Who says there's no such thing as woman's intuition? Hmphh!)

Joe shot a few test photos. Then Sara and Amanda stepped back and discussed the jewelry I was wearing: too much? too little? We chatty friends ran to my jewelry box as Joe scurried around a little more. When we returned, Joe took another test photo. Then the real shooting began. Chin up. Chin down. Legs straight out. Feet crossed. Me draped across the sofa. Me sitting up straight. Hands touching my face. Hands by my side. Put on my jacket. Take off my jacket. All that contortion made me feel like a pretzel, but the attention was enough to make me feel like a spoiled rotten movie star.

Once, when I mentioned how much I like music, Amanda suggested we set the mood, so I found a nice Enya selection. After that played through, I switched to the radio. Well, I like Toby Keith just as much as the next person, but the melody somehow didn't jive with this glamour shot, even though the lyrics of "How Do You Like Me Now?" were kind of cool, wouldn't you say? So, it was bye-bye Toby. Then it was bye-bye, Sara and Amanda. After two hours, they had other places to be. Joe finished up after another hour and we reviewed the CD photos on his laptop. I was astonished. Surely that could not be me, I thought. This man is a miracle worker. I could hardly wait to hear the publisher's (Pam De Grood) reaction.

Joe called me a couple of days later, saying Pam was quite happy with the photos…but one small detail wasn't working. One of my pillows (remember, according to Russell, I have seventy-five or so pillows inside my four-bedroom home) was too busy and therefore, distracting. He asked if could he re-shoot. "Of course," I said.

He came to my home again, and after going through the entire set-up, he snapped for another three hours. Midway through, I asked Joe, "Come to think of it, don't you think the left side of my face looks better than the right side?" (I once saw a doctor on TV say that no human has a perfectly symmetrical face, and we all have a "better" side.) To this, Joe said (being the patient, perfectionist photographer that he is, and did I mention polite?) he could go along with that, although it would involve rearranging the sofa and matching chair. And, without hesitation, he began doing just that. Of course, I chipped in to help. I posed in all those pretzel positions again while he shot photos. I'm not exactly saying I was stiff and needed a chiropractic visit when he left, but I am saying it took a couple of days for my hip bones to remember they were connected to my leg bones. You get the picture? Hey, it's all in a day's work when modeling as a cover girl.

In a store recently, imagine my sheer giddiness to see the likes of me right beside Oprah and Julia Roberts, on their magazine covers in the store shelves. And now it seems, everywhere I go, someone asks me, "Are you on the cover of *GS Magazine?*" where upon I strike a little pose, turning just so, with the left side of my face highlight-ed. Then I smile and say, "Why, sure! How do you like me now?"

CHAPTER 2

Men and Women:
Sharing Worlds, But
from Distant Planets

What's Mine Is Mine and What's His Is Mine (Or Is It?)

Remember as a kid when you and your girlfriends wanted a private place to meet where you could dream, giggle, and tell secrets? So you'd build a tree fort in the woods or drape a sheet over a clothesline. Most important, you'd post a sign that read, "No boys allowed." Flash forward thirty-something years, where in my current home, Russell has just created his own private space. There is no sign that reads, "No girls allowed," but it is implied.

It all began innocently enough one day when Russell announced he wanted a room of his own. I was all for it from the beginning. Heck, I even encouraged the idea. Since my office is directly next to our great room, I would often hear the TV or conversations if Katie and her friends were here—a big distraction. I would end up shutting my office door, only to feel claustrophobic, even left out. But the room Russell settled on, the music room, is farther away. He said this would be his "manly man room."

Next, he bought a TV, DVD, and VCR. Other changes ensued. We moved out the two Queen Anne chairs to the great room, which instantly became my "girly girl room." The new ensemble—two chairs and our contemporary red sofa and oversized matching red chair—blended well with the overall style of our home, which is quite eclectic. (That's a fancy way of saying that nothing matches.)

This same eclectic style began evolving in Russell's new room—the focal point being a Duncan Phyfe sofa, upholstered in a burgundy stripe-on-stripe silk-like pattern. (I would discover later that Russell forbid anything else remotely that formal or frou-frou, but accepted the sofa because it was a family heirloom.) The piano also remained in the room because that too was cherished; Katie plays it when she comes home from college.

From the very beginning, Russell announced about his room, "No girly girl stuff in here, only manly man stuff." (Whatever that means.) As usual, I pretty much ignored him. At some point, we moved two wicker chairs and a swivel rocker into the room. But none of the material matched the sofa. That's when I started shopping for new fabric.

When Russell returned home that night, he exclaimed, "Oh no! Not that again!" "What?" I asked. He glared at the couple of one-hundred-pound bolts of fabric, draped across the chairs, then exclaimed that he didn't even like the patterns. Why was I not surprised? He snubbed the regal gold/purple/red paisley, calling it "feminine." Trying a totally different approach, I asked him what he thought of the green/gold/bronze monkeys, elephants, and lions. I couldn't understand what he was saying through his evil monster-like laugh, though I believe I heard him mumble the word "zoo."

Later, I attempted a more subdued pattern, a tiny-checked gold, nubby one. He muttered that this choice was a little bit better, but only a little bit. Next, I showed him a pale celery-green linen with huge banana leaves, sporting a splash of burgundy. He got downright arrogant, saying, "No flowers in my room." I reminded him that banana plants don't have flowers. Honestly!

We were slowly making progress, so I decided it was time to accessorize the room. We'd start by hanging pictures on the walls. This silly man went nuts and refused to let me hang two famous Anne Worsham Richardson prints of redheaded woodpeckers—one perched on a magnolia, the other on a snow-covered branch—bringing up the no flowers rule again. To add insult to injury, he insisted the prints didn't go with his theme. His *theme?* Undaunted, I sneaked in a colorful Matisse print of a woman playing a guitar. He had a fit! He wouldn't explain why, but I suspect he considered it "girl" artwork, even though I tried pointing out the nice banana-like leaves (by now, he was warming up to that design) in the background. He just shook his head.

After that, Russell quite literally took matters in his own hands. He hurled the banana-leaf fabric bolt to a corner, sighed in exasperation, and pointed to the unmatched chair. "Sit down," he said to me. I knew this was serious and did as I was told. He explained that he didn't want anything in his room with "feathers, fur, boas, beads, crystals, silk, chintz, or brocade"—okay, he didn't say brocade, but I knew what he meant. Then he added, "And no plants!" I challenged this final censorship, but his reply was that plants obstruct his view. (Do not!) And, he said, they have to be watered. (As if he would be the one!)

So here we are, months after designating and decorating his new room and nothing has been re-upholstered. Heck, he never has told me what his theme is. Still, all in all, I suppose I should feel blessed that he allowed me to hang Kelly's bridal portrait, Katie's high school graduation picture, and my recent photo on the cover of *G.S. Magazine*, that my father had framed—all women—in his "manly man room." Oh, he did add a favorite photo to the collection: the one of him and Arnold Palmer playing golf in Latrobe, Pennsylvania, August 1996—his treasured keepsake. And, to his credit, he even allowed me to hang a huge whimsical Christmas print by Ann Hughes Johnson, a family friend.

The room is slowly coming together. In fact, I recently overheard Russell tell a friend that his room is decorated with the greatest people in the world: his wife, his daughters, Arnold Palmer, and Santa Claus. At least he has a sense of humor.

All of this his room/her room has put things in perspective. True, I now have my own room, complete with comfy furniture, a TV, stereo, and all my frilly frou stuff. I have my own space. He has his own space. But something is missing. It's the coziness of being together. You see, now I realize it's not what is in the room; it's who is in the room that counts. Often these days, I end up in his room, reading, watching TV, or talking on the phone (where I promptly get hushed). Sometimes I even snuggle up to him.

I suppose it's true—absence really does make the heart grow fonder. That, and his TV has a much clearer screen, but don't tell him I said so. He just might send me back to the "girly girl room."

Training the Remaining
80% of Men to Clean

This just in. Not exactly a news flash, but rather a news article. I recently read of an interesting study dealing with men and chores. I know! Men and chores in the same article? That's an oxymoron, wouldn't you say? How can that be since you rarely see men and chores in the same *house*, much less the same article? It went on to say that 20% of men report they perform housework, such as cleaning or laundry, versus a *vast majority* (98%, I'm guessing) of women who perform housework. This Very Official Poll from The Ohio State University Extension Service says men would need to perform 60% more housework to catch up to the current household workload of women. Now we're talking! Score one for the women.

Not that I'm trying to cause a major world war here. I'm merely agreeing, while adding my personal observation, which is far more right-on. Most of the men I know would rather buy Coors Lite than Clorox. Most would prefer to dine out than do dishes. And most would rather disappear than dust.

In our house, however, the 20% rule is about right. Hubby Russell is the Official Vacuumer (that's about 20% of the chores). I've always appreciated his manly-man ability to wield that seemingly one-hundred-pound Eureka Bagless Cyclone in record-breaking time in and out of tight nooks and crannies; unlike me, because I run into walls and furniture, and the job takes me half a day.

But now I read (from this same article) that Russell's not the only one vacuuming. It seems that when men are confronted with household chores, the greatest majority will indeed pick vacuuming. And again, though I thought Russell was just being nice, I was sort of surprised at this quote from Randy Sandlin, director of industrial design for Eureka, who said, "It's not like you can vacuum wrong because the vacuum does all the work." Do you think?

Well, how about this? The same thing can be said for mopping the kitchen floor, scrubbing the toilet, and dusting the furniture. According to those savvy commercials, the products do all the work, anyway, not the person, be it man or woman, using the product. You merely guide the mop, brush, or rag as the deep-penetrating, super-power, built-in action knocks the job out in lickety split time.

Further into this article, author Tom McNulty is mentioned. He wrote a book with this enigmatic title, *Clean Like a Man: Housekeeping for Men (And the Women Who Love Them)*. McNulty says men "have no idea where to start, what tools to use, or how to do it right. Basically, we're confused, frustrated, and intimidated." Hogwash! I can't imagine a woman getting by with this arcane, whiney excuse. It's not like we're asking men to rebuild an engine in a Corvette. It's housecleaning, guys.

If a man—at least, my man—can figure out how to play eight-een holes of golf; keep up with the birdies, pars, and bogies; choose the right clubs consistently; and add up the total score, he can certainly handle household chores. Here's a hint: You just do it. I can name that tune (or chore list) in ten seconds and here it is:

Broom, dustpan, mop, cleaner. Sponge, brush, bathroom all-purpose cleaner. Dusting spray and rag. Glass cleaner and paper towels. There you have it. Don't be intimidated, guys. For goodness sake, what would Martha Stewart, the domestic diva, have to say about all of this? Not, "It's a good thing!" After all, she's been teaching us for years how to maintain the perfect home. Of course, you notice she doesn't have a man right now (at least if she does, up-to-the-minute *People* magazine hasn't said so and *People* would know, right?). Come to think of it, maybe that's why Martha doesn't have a man. She couldn't find one trained to clean.

The Thrill of the Hunt— for Him and Her

A revelation came to me the other day, with it being late fall and cooler weather setting in, inciting one more difference between men and women. Hunting. But the more I thought about it, the more I realized we humans are all born hunters, not just men. It's true. All across America, men and women are preparing right now for their particular hunt: Men are buying hunting licenses (depending on the locale and date, it might be for deer, quail, dove, or duck), but women are also preparing. The slight difference is we women aren't searching for wild animals; we're searching for wild bargains. And though we don't have a paper hunting license, we often have a plastic hunting license, a.k.a. Master"Charred," American Express, Visa, and Discover, followed closely by our debit cards. And when all else fails, the green stuff—cash.

I've noticed that this male hunting frenzy can be complicated or simple. Case in point, a few days ago, a gym buddy described to me his upcoming trip to a hunting club in the Deep South, which was once a rice plantation. By day, he and his friends dress in hunting attire to hunt for quail. By night, they "dress to the nines" when dinner is served on fine china promptly at 8 p.m. They also have comfy rooms, each with their own full bath and wet bar. They are waited on hand and foot, and want for nothing. Out in "the wild," they are led to their prey by hunting dogs and/or horses.

Though my husband is not a hunter (Russell is a golfer), my father is, so I'm familiar with Dad's routine. He has spent winters past in Gunnison, Colorado, hunting for elk; and in Sheridan, Montana, hunting for antelope. Dad has to "apply" for these hunts a year in advance, by way of a lottery—a smart and sound environmental plan, which ensures the wildlife population is not depleted. If he is lucky enough to be selected, Dad pores over Cabelos and L.L. Bean catalogs, ordering the latest gear and gizmos to make his journey complete. He awaits the big day much like a child at Christmas. These are examples of complicated hunts.

On the other hand, my brother-in-law Keith does things much simpler. He just calls up a hunting buddy late on a Thursday night and makes plans over a cold beer and a fat cigar. Twelve hours later, Keith is driving to a duck blind (in his rusty, old pick-up truck). Later, he'll be heard saying, "Sheezam! Ju'see that?" Then they come home stinky and sweaty, bleary-eyed and exhausted, but proud of their prize: a duck, a quail, whatever, which they promptly stick in their freezers and their wives promptly ignore, because most of the women I know have no desire to cook that stuff. Ever.

Running parallel, the female hunting experience can also be complicated or simple. Some women mark Thanksgiving as the beginning of their hunting season. They make plans months ahead to fly to New York, D.C., or Atlanta with the girls. While there, they dine at their favorite five-star restaurants, take in a play or two, and map out their strategy to hit Macy's, Neiman Marcus, and Saks Fifth Avenue sales. All shopped out, spent out, and worn out, they return home with their prizes: Christmas gifts.

On a simpler scale, I call my friend Carolyn the night before and say, "Did you know Dillard's is having an early-bird sale tomorrow?" In less than twelve hours, we're inside the store, bumping into the other dazed-and-crazed shoppers, filling up buggies faster than you can sing the first line of "Silver Bells." This activity is, of course, followed by a gourmet lunch. (See, that's another thing men and women have in common. We love to eat, but we love for someone else to do the cooking.)

Another notation within this hunting arena is that woman and men seem to have the same goals: to spend quality time with good friends, enjoy exciting and stimulating conversation, and come home with something we're proud of. Call it a hobby, R&R, or downtime, but we all need a diversion from the hustle and hassle of stress from work, family, health, and financial issues.

I have noticed, however, one major difference in the male/female hunting comparison, that being the lingo. For example, they're standing in duck blinds, and we're standing at sidewalk sales. They're loaded for bear, and we're loaded for bargains. They're staying at the hunting club, and we're staying at the Hyatt Regency. They're wearing Rocky boots, and we're wearing Nikes 'cause, everybody hear me now, *when your feet hurt, you hurt all over!* They're sporting a Remington 30-06; we're sporting a Ralph Lauren 20x30 purse. They might bag a deer, but our bag also holds something dear. They're talking thrill of the hunt; we're talking thrill of the sale—70% off of half price, plus 20% markdown at the register (before 11 a.m.), and a coupon for an additional 10% means it's practically free.

Yeah, the more I think about it, men may be from Mars and women may be from Venus (to borrow the title of the book by John Gray), but this is also true: Men may like hunting and traipsing through the woods, but women like shopping and bringing home the goods. Happy hunting, all!

I Can't Abide with a Man
"In Touch with His Feminine Side"

What's all this talk about today's woman being attracted to a man "in touch with his feminine side"? What exactly does that mean? That these men love to shop, enjoy gossip, and cry easily? My feminine side is in touch with prairie skirts, stacked heels, and red fingernails. These aren't qualities I would enjoy seeing in a man. Why in the world would a woman be attracted to a man who gets turned on by listening to Michael Bolton love songs and wearing multiple silver bangle bracelets? That's a girl thing. Being with a man like this would be like staring into a reflection of ourselves. I don't think so, sugar. This is where the phrase "opposites attract" comes in to play.

Remember the Equal Rights Amendment that we fought so hard for in the late 1970s and early '80s? We wanted to be treated equally then and we still do today. But we're losing ground (as well as our minds) if we think men need to be more like us. It's plenty fine to stop with equality as in equal pay, treatment, and rights. But not equal genes. They're not equal and they never will be.

I'm sorry, but I don't want my hubby sitting next to me bawling during chick flicks, testing perfumes in lingerie shops, and asking "How do I look, honey?" while wearing Manolo pumps. Anyway, whenever we women ask "How do I look, honey?" the men always say, "Just like you always do." Next, we end up pouting (our feminine side). And they end up clueless (their masculine side). It's too scary discussing subjects like lash tints and eyebrow waxing with a man giggling at your side. And it's for sure that men can't relate to PMS, childbirth, and menopause. Next thing you know they'll want to borrow our black bras and silk scarves. No way! That's what girl-friends do, and we don't need or want to replace them.

I want my man to be in touch with *his* masculine side, not *my* feminine side, thank you very much. Men can keep living like they always have, discussing prostate trouble and radiator problems with the guys, standing around the campfire, preparing for a buffalo hunt (or whatever they hunt). It's worked for eons. Why change now?

I'm keeping my eye on these metropolitan men called "metro-sexuals" to be make certain they don't cross the line and take over our previously dominated world of hairstylists, manicurists, and massage therapists. Next thing you know, we women won't even be able to get appointments—the men will have them all booked. Remember, women, we were here first. We have separate locker rooms at the gym and there's a reason for that. Sitting in the lobby of the local salon and spa reading articles from *Cosmo* and other magazines with titles like "Fifty Secrets to Make Your Man Beg for More" is personal. We need our personal space; men do, too (so long as it's not located in the same building as ours). Maybe I'm a salon snob but this is the best place in the world to discuss *men*—who George Clooney is dating this month, Ty Pennington's newest re-modeling project, or whether "The Bachelor" tied the knot. It's a lot easier to gossip about men when they aren't present to interrupt or defend themselves.

I believe females are supposed to be feminine and males are sup-posed to be masculine: *F* for female (feminine) and *m* for male (mas-culine). How would it sound if President George Bush became President Georgia Bush? Bill Gates became Billie Jean Gates? Steve Spurrier became Stephanie Spurrier? Not too good, huh?

That doesn't mean the two genders can't overlap some. But I want my husband to be my husband, not an extension of me, not a reminder of my mother, and not a girlfriend. He needs to be a com-plete package with manly tendencies, pulsating testosterone and the whole nine yards. This includes but is not limited to hair stubble on the face, large biceps, and decent abilities with tools. Nothing wrong with that as far as I can see.

With that in mind, it makes me wonder if these pro-"men in touch with their feminine side" women are a few points shy of nor-mal on the old IQ score. It's like this: Have you ever heard a man say he's attracted to a woman who's "in touch with her masculine side?" I didn't think so. I rest my case.

Oscar & Prissy: The Original Power-Struggle Couple

In our family of nineteen adults and children, we've just learned that a twentieth will soon be added. My nephew Huck Huxley is engaged to marry Heather Reid. With all those H's, won't their monogrammed towels be stunning? This is thrilling news for everyone, especially my sister Nancy, who is Huck's mother. I'm contemplating what sage advice I can offer or what poignant quotes I can recite during the champagne toast at the rehearsal dinner.

I started out by asking myself "What is marriage?" In the traditional term, is it the blending of two lives and two hearts? Or philosophically, is it "Joy in the Morning"? I always did like that song. Or is it technically a partnership, a union, a bond that tells the world, "We are one"? Nope, 'fraid not. I've decided the real truth is that *it's closer to being a power struggle* than anything else. It's like being at one of those chaotic events when someone finally yells, "Who's in charge here?" except marriage lasts much, much longer.

In fairness, here's how we've worked it out. One day I'm in charge and the next day, dear Russell (known to me as *Oscar the Grouch*) is in charge. Or at least he thinks he is. And that, girlfriends, is the secret to happily-wedded bliss: today you're in charge and tomorrow he's in charge. Only thing is, tomorrow never comes!

Oscar and I (nicknamed *Prissy Pollyanna* by hubby) have been married for twenty-five years, and we've been through every kind of power struggle you can imagine—from the thermostat setting in our home (Oscar says sixty-five in the winter and seventy-five in the summer) to figuring out directions while traveling (Prissy says *buy a map*). So now, let me list a few power struggles we've had over the years and share how we've settled them. Heather and Huck, honey, are you listening?

Supposedly, most couples argue over money, chores, sex, and children. I'll address only the first two because the other two haven't been a problem for us. (We've had sex and we've had children. Duh!)

With the money part, Oscar has lots of silly ideas. When I shop, he always grills me afterwards with, "How much money did you save me?" then starts to defend his personal position of *NMNB*, or No Money, No Buy. What I try to explain to him is that I *do* have money. I mean, after all, I have checks in my checkbook, some charge cards, and when all else fails, Ready-Reserve. I've got money. (Heather, if you're smart, you'll recite that same mantra.)

Oscar also supports living within one's means. Yeah, well, I tried that too, but it only ended up costing me more in the long run. When I walked into a store, I'd try to save money by scoping the place out for sale signs, which are always above the clothes racks, which are always above my short 5' 4" frame. Later, I'd have aching muscle spasms down my neck and shoulders, culminating in emergency visits to the chiropractor. (Heather, because you are way taller than me, you can say you had to look down at the signs, and see if that'll fly.)

Oscar also points out the ridiculous Oscar-designed three-way test: 1) Do you need it? 2) Can you afford it? 3) Can you live without it? After careful consideration, I always come up with the same three answers: yes, yes, no. (Heather, if you're smart, say the same thing. Don't think this over too long or change any answers.)

Now we'll move on to the subject of chores. My rule is, if I cook, Oscar cleans up, though it's true he complains a lot. Oscar recently whined, "We only had three things for dinner tonight and they were leftovers! How did you mess up all these pots and pans?" Undaunted, I made large sweeping gestures as I told him, "Silly boy, see here, I made potato pancakes out of leftover mashed potatoes. I made a cheese sauce for leftover broccoli. And I opened a jar of gravy to pour over the leftover roast chicken. That way, nothing tasted like leftovers." He holds up his hand, as if to say, "Stop." (He shouldn't ask if he doesn't truly want to know.) He reminds me, "Prissy, that's why they're called leftovers! They're *supposed* to taste like leftovers." Well, I hate leftovers. Finally he whines, "Well, it's not fair." My reply is, "Oscar, life is not fair. Get over it." (Heather, this last phrase is a catch-all for anything you disagree on.)

Another piece of advice: Use playful nicknames like Honey or Sweetie to describe your spouse. Though "Oscar" isn't a playful name, it's well chosen, and, well, I guess Prissy Pollyanna is on the mark, too. Can I help it if I'm gullible and I look on the bright side of things (for example, underneath the black cloud that constantly forms over Oscar's head)? And sure, I sway my hips when I walk and bat my eyelashes when I speak. So what? In many parts of the world these are considered desirable traits. And if Oscar says I'm Prissy because I love self indulgences like new hairstyles, manicures, massages, frou-frou clothes, diva shoes, and awesome jewelry...well, then, he's right.

However, some men, the aforementioned metrosexuals, are also spending big bucks getting pampered at previously held women's turf—nail salons and spas, for instance. Since big bucks are what it takes, rest assured, Oscar will forego that. He is perfectly content with his $8 barbershop buzz cut, his $2 Fruit of the Loom's, and as for nails, fuhgetaboutit because he bites them down to the quick regularly. And massages are definitely out because Oscar is ticklish and laughs hysterically when touched. (So, Huck, *not that I would pick sides*, but if you decide to spend big bucks as a metrosexual, just remember that Heather holds the power today, and you hold it tomorrow.)

So to Huck and Heather—and all the newlywed couples out there—congratulations and best wishes. And a big congratulations to the long-together couples, too, because you've earned it. Here's to a happy and powerful marriage year after year!

All About Russell, a Wannabe Boy Scout

Russell has turned into a Boy Scout. Oh, not officially, but he is starting to remind me of one. For one thing he's ready for a camp out on a moment's notice. On any given night, he hops into bed with either a long-sleeved turtleneck and sweatpants (on those bitter nights when the temperature drops into the teens) or a golf shirt and sweat shorts (if the weather is a little milder). I keep asking him if he plans to sneak out in the middle of the night, but he just snickers and says, "Very funny." I check to be sure he doesn't have his shoes on (under the covers) and he doesn't, but he does have on thick socks. Hmmm.

I have tried to buy that man a pair of real *pajamas* for as long as we've been married, but he won't have any part of it. In fact, he gets downright nasty when I bring it up. "Won't wear 'em. You'd be wasting your money. You know I *hate* pajamas." I don't get it. (I, on the other hand, love night clothes!) I'm not sure if he thinks real men don't wear pajamas, or else he equates wearing them with little old granddaddies. Wait a minute. He *is* a granddaddy. But Russell is not little or old.

I almost sneaked in a pajama purchase for him right before one Christmas, but Russell was on to my scheming and it didn't work. He had some plantar warts removed via the Q-tip-dipped-in-acid method in November, and his foot doctor told him to go home and rest. That night he came home, soaked his feet in hot soapy water, and the next thing I knew—watch out! He was hobbling around in some polyester bedroom slipper-things that someone had given him a few years back as a joke. These "shoes" didn't even have a heel, but rather were white papery-thin, slide-looking objects that had a golf shoe tassel drawn on them. He literally glided, as opposed to walked, in them. They were so slippery he came right out of them several times. That, coupled with the pain medicine he was taking (which caused him to walk funny anyway) was truly a sight for sore eyes; or in his case, a sight for sore feet. Poor guy.

The next day I decided to drive to my favorite department store and surprise him by buying him some attractive, well-made, cushioned leather bedroom slippers. That night at home he tried them on, but disappointingly announced they were too small. In fact, they were an even worse choice than that pair he'd worn the night before. So, off we went together the next day to exchange them. It was then that I located a beautiful pair of pajamas to match the slippers. When I showed them to him in the store he gave me *the look*, shook his head, then glanced at his watch and told me to hurry, he was missing The Skins Game on TV.

The other Boy Scout thing he's become quite fond of is the bonfire. He burnt some trash after raking our yard a few months back and now that's all he can talk about. He actually walks around the house and yard in search of things to burn. We've even had a few words over this.

One day I found him removing things from my official Garage Sale Pile to put in his official Bonfire Pile. The day of the meltdown (the first bonfire) he gathered his limbs, leaves, and logs, and threw a match on the heap. Russell had of course secured his burning permit first, and there was no wind in sight, so it was perfectly safe. It was a cool, clear day. Pretty soon he was out there stoking that fire like it was his prized possession. This is the same man who will not build a fire in our fireplace because he says it's too much trouble and it doesn't last long enough, whatever that means. (I guess playing a round of golf six hours does last long enough.)

Then there is the fingernail thing, which is more Amazon creature-like than Boy Scout-like. This next part is gross, so skip over it if you're faint of heart. As I've mentioned before, he has this annoying habit of biting his fingernails and spitting them out. They land in the most awful places: on the end table where I serve my guests coffee or tea. Or else in my car, trapped on the floor between the passenger's seat and the car door. It's disgusting. When I ask him to please use clippers like everyone else, he asks, "Why?" He thinks that's what teeth are for. I could go on and on. (Of course, I have no loathsome, undesirable, uncouth personal habits, so it's easy for me to pick on Russell.)

I finally came right out and asked him the other day if he was ever a Boy Scout. To my surprise, he said yes, he was a Cub Scout for about six months. He even wore a uniform. But he never got to go on a camping trip, build a bonfire, roast marshmallows, or go fishing. (He still won't go fishing and I know, because I've asked him to go with me.) Upon further questioning, he told me he'd won some badges way back then, but he can't remember what they were for. He did say he had trouble hitting a nail in a board, but still managed to get his carpenter badge. Funny! Mr. Fixer Upper, he is not.

Anyway, I've got him analyzed now about the pajamas and the bonfire, but the fingernails have me stumped. Maybe he had to peel away the bark barehanded before he hammered the nail in the board some forty years ago. Yeah, that would have been tough with untrimmed fingernails. Bet that surely could hurt—the wood under the nails—a lot worse than those creepy plantar warts.

From Teen Idol to OB/GYN: Dr. Barbie-Doll Sure Gets My Attention!

Where have I been? I had no idea that Barbie, my favorite doll from childhood, had grown up and become a doctor. It's true. It says so right here in Target's "Expect More, Pay Less" flier that arrived in my newspaper this morning along with sixteen other circulars. (I counted.) I had planned on doing something really useful today, like vacuuming out my refrigerator motor coils, but now I see I'll be busy perfecting the family budget, while reading how much money I can save at the local stores.

Getting back to *Dr. Barbie*. Doesn't that just have a precious ring to it? I realize my children are grown and gone, so it stands to reason that no one would have told me this catchy news. Still, I would have appreciated a warning. Instead, I turned to page thirteen and there she was, in her pink printed doctor's smock holding newborn twins. Twins! And of course, she is not without a friend, albeit a patient, Midge. (Now that's a really popular name these days, huh? Right up there with Britney, Taylor, and McKenzie—*what was Mattel thinking?*) And Midge is just as pregnant as she can be, though she's styling. Oh yes. She is wearing a sweet Lily-look-alike pink and purple dress with a charming bow tied at her empire waistline, and fashionable hot-pink heels to match—great for swollen feet and ankles at about eight months along. And her hair! Well, that's a curious anomaly. We are talking straight-as-a-stick golden locks flowing down past her thigh-high panty line. How ever does she brush it? I could be wrong, but isn't the hemline of her tiny frock about four full inches above her knees?

That's okay, let's just move on to Daddy Alan. What can I say, except that he is scary looking. He has a strange resemblance to a crash-test dummy that was just zapped with a stun gun, but not before he signed a multi-dollar modeling contract. Alan's expression is an absurd mixture of fear and ecstasy combined. I wonder if his emotional state has anything to do with his hyped-up, giddy toddler, Ryan, who also has that "I'm a star" grin. And get this: Daddy and son are dressed identical in their blue plaid zip-up shirt and khaki shorts. What the heck kind of style is this? Maybe Scandinavian, but I've never seen it around my town. And that precious bowl-cut "Dorothy Hamil" mop of hair that Ryan sports sure sets him apart from the other tykes.

But back to Barbie again—oh, forgive me, *Dr.* Barbie (have a bit of respect, after all). It has been over forty years since Jane Summerlin (my neighbor and best friend) and I sat under a maple tree, spread out a blanket, and allowed our Barbies to play together. I wish I had that doll now to add to my proudest collections, right beside my McCoy Aunt Jemima cookie jar. Who would have guessed then what a great future Barbie had ahead of her? Jane and I were about eight years old, and our Barbies were about eighteen, so of course we really looked up to them, and yet, we were the bosses. We could decide what they would wear, where they would go, and who their friends would be. We hadn't even thought about husbands for them way back then, but we sure had fun letting them play the field.

But hey, it looks like old Barb ended up doing really well with no input from us. From the looks of things, I'd say she must have married a gifted plastic surgeon. That would be Ken, right? I mean who else could have erased those horrid bird's-eye wrinkles from around her brilliantly clear blue eyes, or eliminated those sagging chicken neck folds? Then again, maybe it was her hairdresser who specializes in hair implants. After all, she's got a bushel basket full of this straw-colored stuff that flips up, ever so cute.

Maybe I'm wrong. Perhaps it was her personal trainer, considering that petite size four figure she so proudly displays. Bless her heart, she hasn't changed at all. She's still perfect. Yes, she's been through a lot of different careers in her lifetime, but I think OB/GYN is the smartest one she's picked. Dr. Barbie has the freshest, happiest, dreamiest look on her face that I've ever seen.

A final glimpse at the ad leaves me curious, though. It reads,

"Each [doll] comes with fun accessories." If I sit real still and let my imagination run wild, I can bet what those items might be: Midge's million-dollar Malibu mansion. Alan's audacious Atlantic Avenue accounting office, and Barbie's bodacious baby bungalow-clinic.

Wait a minute, did the ad say fun? Well, now that's a different story altogether. My guess is those fun accessories, as in real life, are for the men only. While Dr. Barbie is busy delivering babies and Midge is busy birthing babies, Dad and son are off in la-la land, strolling around in their comfy Skechers with their silly devil-may-care attitude and goofy smiles. You know, this replica of life is getting more real by the minute.

Rainy Days and Birthdays Always Get Him Down

Birthdays are meant to be joyous occasions where the honoree is sung to, presented gifts, and fed birthday cake. This was not the case, recently, for hubby, Russell. But it was his own fault since he chose golf over cake!

I know for a fact that Russell is sensitive about his birthday, ever since his mama forgot his seventeenth birthday. He's told me the story many times of how he daydreamed all afternoon about that scrumptious cake his mama was baking for him, while he was cropping tobacco that sweltering summer. But when he got home, his anticipation gave way to disappointment. There was no cake. Mama had plumb forgotten. When he started singing "Happy Birthday" to himself, she gasped. She felt terrible, especially since she was a part-time caterer and was known far-and-wide for her legendary cakes. She made it up to him though, by baking his favorite cake the next day. Still, he never let her forget that blunder.

I haven't been much better in the remembering department. One time I remembered his present, but forgot his card. So I looked through my basket of "just in case" cards—the oddball ones that I'd bought simply because they were on sale, the artwork was catchy, or the message was touching. Russell was excitedly ripping the bow off my gift, when I hollered, "Wait!" He grimaced as I ran down the hall. I grabbed a card that read, "Happy Birthday to a dear friend." I quickly marked out "friend" and wrote over it, "husband."

Another year I gave him a card that I'd given him the year before. I wouldn't have believed it if he hadn't rummaged through a drawer and pulled out the old card for proof. At least my taste is consistent. And yes, my new handwritten message *was* different.

This year, I baked Russell his favorite birthday cake. Well, actually, it's not a cake at all, but rather one large, dense chocolate brownie. People look at you funny if you say "birthday brownie," so I don't.

It's like this: ooey, gooey, and truffle-like, thanks to the rich ingredients of butter, eggs, chocolate, and whipping cream. One bite and you can actually feel your waist expanding—or almost. I baked the cake the day before his birthday, for the flavors to meld. In the meantime, my dear aunt Shirley called that night, asking me what I'd been up to. I described in detail the "cake" I'd just made. Then I offered to bring her some. Through salivating, garbled language, she said, "I'd wuv some!" I was caught up in the moment, not realizing that the cake would then be lopsided. I cut the square cake into four sections and took her one-fourth.

The next day, when it came time for the "party," I asked Kelly, our oldest daughter, to write a message on the cake with the store-bought tube of squirtable icing. She's a kindergarten teacher and has a lovely handwriting. One look at this cake, which was now shaped like a big fat "L," with messy cut marks, and Kelly scowled. Sensing her despair, I used my fingers to "glue" the icing back together over the lines; but it just made things worse. Now it was bumpy, unequal, and uneven. Remarkably, Kelly was able to write R-U-S-S-E-L-L at the larger bottom portion of the cake. But there was no room for H-A-P-P-Y B-I-R-T-H-D-A-Y across the smaller top portion. She could only fit in H. B'Day.

We didn't have enough candles (or room) for his age, so instead we placed five on top and two on bottom to represent fifty-two. Kelly handed out plates, forks, and napkins on the back porch. I found a festive dish to help with the presentation of the pitiful-looking cake, and lit the candles. Kelly opened the door. I stepped out and lead everyone—daughter Katie, my parents, my brother, his wife, and their son—in singing "Happy Birthday." Madison, our three-year-old granddaughter, helped Russell extinguish the scant candles and open his gifts. Next, we started handing out cake.

Russell surprised us by saying he'd wait for his piece as he was full from lunch. Plus, he was worried about predicted rains, and wanted to hurry out to the golf course. Of course, no one else wanted to save the cake for later. We all sat there, piggedly stuffing down the chocolate concoction, celebrating Russell's birthday without a care in the world...and, obviously, without him.

Afterwards, I put the cake in the refrigerator and didn't give it much thought. Evidently, some other folks *did*. I'm thinking there might have even been some covert snacking going on behind my back. Later that night Russell said, "I believe I'll have a piece of my cake now." "Uh oh," I said in earnest, "I hope there's a piece left." That's exactly what I found when I opened the fridge. One small piece. It had the squished and melted letter "L" left from his printed name, but it looked more like a quarter-moon. I decided in this case, "L" stood for "Lucky," because he was lucky it wasn't all gone.

Looking back, I wonder if our group celebrated the first birthday in history where the honoree got the last piece of his own cake. Everyone else sure enjoyed the party, though. And I'll bet that next year, golf or no golf, rain or no rain, Russell will grab a piece when he's first offered. I also learned for future reference that if you're going to give away cake before the party starts, simply trim around the edges, to form a nice neat circle. This should leave plenty of room for the entire message and all the candles.

Iron and Steel (But Not Russell's Duke Aluminum Can) Make My Kitchen Complete

I never feel more powerful or alive than when I'm in my own kitchen, frying—er, make that sautéing—food in my ten-inch, cast iron skillet, or when wielding my eight-inch high-carbon stainless-steel knife. The skillet is older than me (no surly comments, please) and the knife is my newest culinary gizmo.

Almost nightly I use both the knife and the skillet. I cook with lots of garlic and fresh herbs, so it makes sense that I slice, dice, and sauté. Also, being a member of three supper clubs, a cookbook collector, and a regular Food Channel viewer, I pride myself in owning the newest gadgets on the market—though I'm *still* holding out on a stand-alone mixer to replace the old hand-held model that randomly spits out one beater when mixing. "Oh dear, another beater in the batter" is my mantra. I yell this above the clicking off-balance remaining beater, but my hints go unnoticed by family members.

I've always loved kitchen supply stores. Give me a wall of juicers, strainers, reamers, and steamers and I'm grinning like a Cheshire cat. Some people dream of winning the lottery; I'd be thrilled with a $500 shopping spree at Williams-Sonoma. After all, true culinary masters know half the fun of cooking is searching for the right tools.

I didn't buy my cast iron skillet. I got it the old-fashioned way: I inherited it from Granny Pinky. That skillet was Granny's prized possession. If skillets could talk, this one would share tales of hilarious fiascos: scorched fatback, burned cornbread, and overdone fried chicken. (Granny had two settings on her stove: off and high). But the best dish she cooked in that skillet (and one that she never burned) was blueberry cobbler. That frying pan was like a member of our family. It sat on the stove like a good-luck charm—dependable, reassuring, and ever-ready for battle, I mean, service. Granny's skillet never needed seasoning (a modern-day suggestion, as far as I can tell) because it never had a chance to get rusty, gooey, or sticky. It was constantly in use.

Granny's trademark in the kitchen was her skillet; mine has become my big knife. That's what Russell calls it. Quite frankly, he doesn't like the thing. In fact, he abhors it. I'll admit I was a little intimidated the first time I picked it up and tried to mince fresh ginger, what with its razor-sharp blade, intimidating size, and bulky weight. So I watched lots of cooking shows and determined the secret of using it successfully. It's all in the wrist. You must learn to rock the knife back and forth, not picking it up off the cutting board, while keeping the tip of the blade in one spot. And you *must* keep your fingers curled under to avoid nasty accidents.

In fact, I was so proud that I asked Russell to watch me perform my newfound culinary skill I'd mastered, thinking I might even allay his fears. But if anything, he seemed more tense during my demonstration. That's when it dawned on me. It wasn't the knife that worried him; it was the potential danger of *me* holding the knife, klutz that I can be. Either that or he's seen too many Lifetime movies about good women gone bad, involved in criminal activities, missing bodies, and insurance fraud. So I came up with an offer. I'd put away my prized possession (knife) if he'd put away his (aluminum can).

Let me explain. Years ago Russell acquired an unopened Duke True Blue II Soda can, a memento from the 1991–92 NCAA basketball championship. True, it's a food item, but this aluminum atrocity doesn't belong in my kitchen, where he likes it displayed. I'd move it from one spot to another because it never "flowed" with other items (groupings of candles or fruit baskets and certainly not my McCoy cookie jar) and the blue didn't match my green and rust colors. One day, I decided this soda can, my nemesis, had to be removed from the kitchen once and for all. I stuck it in the least used room in our house, the guest room (looking even more hideous on the dresser next to my McCoy vases and dried hydrangeas).

Sad to say, Russell refused my offer. Here's another one. Next time I use my knife, I'll suggest he watch some sports on TV while drinking that vintage Duke soda. Anything to get rid of it!

CHAPTER 3
Hardly the Norm: Accidents and Sheer Wonders

Good Night, Sleep Tight, But Beware— the Bedbugs May Bite!

I've got disturbing news for Martha Stewart, Rachel Ashwell, Katie Brown, and all the other domestic mega-divas. These designers have steered us, heck, they've practically *brainwashed* us, into buying used furniture and junk. Oh, sure, these mavens conveniently smooth over the stale term "used" with more hip-hop terms like vintage, antique, and shabby-chic. But we know the truth: the items are still used. And they're used not only by the previous owners, but quite possibly by the present owners. That being, *bedbugs!*

I know! Go ahead and say, "What, are you crazy? There's no such thing as bedbugs." That's exactly what I said when I read the article in *USA Today.* I thought the word "bedbugs" was simply invented for that old rhyme, "Good night. Sleep tight. Don't let the bedbugs bite." Wrong! Just like chiggers, mites, and lice, not only are bedbugs real, they're a real pain. They're invading our homes, hotels, and haciendas in alarming numbers.

It turns out these welt-producing bloodsuckers were nearly eradicated sixty years ago; but just like Lesley Ann Warren trying to make a comeback on *Desperate Housewives,* they're here to stay, dang it. Maybe bedbugs will have better luck than Lesley, bless her heart. If she wasn't so ditzy, immature, and pathetic, I swear I would like her. Really, I would.

What's even worse about these varmints is they only come out at night, which is terribly inconvenient and annoying, since, well, most humans *sleep* at night. The bugs are so tiny they can even crawl through a stitch-hole in a mattress. I don't know about you, but as soon as I read that part, I went and checked out my mattress, which I never knew had stitch holes. Turns out it does, so I guess I'm not immune either.

Now, don't be too quick to say, "Surely they're not here in South Carolina." Au contraire. Yes they are too, right here in the Palmetto State. And why not? They've got plenty of company with all the other menacing insects our state is known for: mosquitoes, no-seeums, fruit flies, ticks, and fire ants. In fact, there are only seven states that have *not* had bedbugs reported: Idaho, New Hampshire, Rhode Island, Wyoming, Alaska, and North and South Dakota. Here's an idea. The next time your annoying in-laws, ex-business partners, or braggart friends call to come visit you for a week-long visit, you might want to point out this unknown but thought-provoking fact.

And here's some info for you spotless housekeepers who make us sloppy domestics feel inept. (What's the harm in a little ring around my bathtub or fingerprints on the refrigerator from my three-year-old granddaughter who is now four?) The good news/ bad news, depending on how you look at it, is that cleanliness is indeed next to godliness. However, this fact has nothing to do with where bedbugs take up residence.

Case in point: Bedbugs have even turned up at The Helmsley Park Lane Hotel in New York, where a one-bedroom suite runs $950 per night. Funny thing is, it can cost more than a night's stay ($1000) to completely eradicate an infestation of bedbugs once their presence is confirmed. That's because the treatment can require pesticides, powerful vacuums, and sealing mattresses with impervious covers. Eek! This is starting to sound like a horror movie.

Thankfully, these bugs don't spread disease. But all things being equal, how is that going to console someone who gets a case of the bedbugs? In fact, Richard Pollack of the Harvard School of Public Health puts it this way, "If you wake up at 2 a.m. and something's sucking on your ankle, that's a pretty good sign." Honey, if I wake up at 2 a.m. and something is sucking on my ankle, he'd better be tall, dark, and handsome! Well, two out of three isn't bad, which describes Russell. (No one's perfect, right?)

So, the point is (and I do have one) that bedbugs are here to stay, at least for now. Besides the used furniture and bed linens route, they also fly around the world embedded in folk's luggage and travel bags. Wouldn't you just know it? It's been a little over a year since I lost my fear of flying phobia and took to the skies bravely. I've flown more in this last year than all of my previous years combined, tuning out the scary thoughts of bad weather, pilot error, or missed connections. But now I've got a new bugaboo to deal with: bedbugs!

Don't be surprised in the future if a popular TV network talks about the hazards, rather than the benefits, of decorating with other people's furniture and junk. Instead of being HGTV, The Learning Channel, or Style Network, it might just be the Discovery Channel doing a bedbug documentary.

But have no fear, if Martha gets a hold of this, she'll probably figure out a way to recycle, reuse, and refresh with the hard shell left behind—perhaps replacing the goose-down pillow with the bedbug pillow. At least it has a nice sound to it. Wouldn't you agree?

Changing Light Bulbs Can Be Hazardous to Your Health

Talk about a freak accident. Dear Russell recently fell off the bed, onto his head, and landed on his shoulder. Said shoulder turned out later not to be broken, thank God, but separated. Ensuing ice packs, Tylenol, and a shoulder sling have brought some relief. But he's not ready to let it go. He's no fool, since all that extra attention and pity would abruptly end.

Contrary to various wild tales, false accusations, and rumors flying, what happened is actually rather boring. Russell was changing a light bulb in the paddle fan over our bed, perched on his knees. Though the elevated rice-poster cherry bed is more than sturdy, the comforter atop the mattress is dangerously slick.

The crash happened while I was in the bathtub one night, shaving my legs. Hey, it was Saturday night and with church the next day, it's my weekly routine. Sunday Stubble is oh so gauche. As I lay soaking in my herbal-scented bath salts, nearly nodding off to sleep, the loud thud jolted me back to reality. Next came "Arghhhhhhh!" from the adjoining room.

I jumped out of the tub, slipping and sliding on the tile floor, naked as a jaybird, dripping water all over the place. I ran to Russell, who was mysteriously not there. At least, not from the angle where I stood and dripped. I rounded the bed to find him sprawled out on the floor, moaning—feet in the air and face and shoulder jammed into the carpet.

I froze, fearing he'd broken a bone. "Are you all right?" I said, my voice quivering. After a few choice words, he hollered, "No, I'm not all right! Can't you see I fell off the bed?" Then I surprised myself. I am sooooo embarrassed to tell you this. I started crying, though I'm not sure why. In fact, in my family, we women have this sick habit of *laughing* when someone gets hurt. Stump your toe on a piece of furniture? Ha ha! Trip over a heavy box? Tee hee! And if you walk into a cabinet door, *get out!* We become hysterical. I know it's sick.

Obviously annoyed, Russell said, "Why are you crying? I'm the one who's hurt." Good question. I couldn't even answer it myself. But then he rubbed salt into the wound by saying, "I should've never changed that light bulb tonight. This probably would've never happened if I'd waited until tomorrow." Do what? Not very rational, I thought, wondering if he'd hit his head on the way down. No, I'm guessing not, since Russell believes, "Never do today what you can put off 'til tomorrow."

He struggled a moment, then stood up and hobbled towards the door. Drying my eyes, I tenderly asked him if he needed to go to the E.R. He ignored me (perhaps too humiliated and irritated to answer). Noting my one smooth and one stubbly leg, I jumped back into the now chilly bathwater, yelling out, "Put some ice on it! And take some Tylenol!" Hey, I only have so much sympathy in me.

The next morning he woke up in even more pain. He grimaced while struggling to put on his shirt, unable to lift his arm higher than his chest. Later, at church, as luck would have it, a dear friend and orthopedist checked him, saying to come by the office for an X-ray the following day. He wanted to rule out a fracture, though he suspected his shoulder was merely separated. Oh, and he told Russell to put his arm in a sling.

So after lunch we trekked up to the nearest pharmacy, where of all people, our minister's wife and son were inside shopping. Other than the doctor, Sara Dee and Cooper were the first to hear this absurd tale. (I think we realized then we'd hear lots of wise cracks.) But while Sara Dee and I chatted about girl things—a new restaurant, the darling new shoes she had on, and so forth and so on, Russell whined. He waved around the instructions for the sling, pleading for someone to assist him. I marched right over, read the first line, and announced, "I don't understand this." (I never understand directions.) Sweet thing that she is, Sara Dee offered her assistance, while I followed Cooper around the store for a while.

The next day at Russell's weekly staff meeting (he's a church administrator) the jokes flew. What were you really doing in bed? Was it the satin sheets? How many church administrators does it take to change a light bulb? Was this a case of domestic violence? And some were more crass (but I can't repeat them).

Thankfully, there were no broken bones, only a broken spirit. Why? Well, it's not because Russell can't carry me over the threshold like honeymooners do, or give me a fabulous back rub that I do so enjoy. To him, the saddest part is that he can't golf for a month or work out at the gym—he was a lean, mean machine with several months of renewed commitment and serious workouts behind him. That in turn makes my life miserable because he'll be even grumpier than usual!

It's been three weeks since the tumble, and we're heading out of town this weekend. I noticed he sneaked his golf putter in the back seat which ought to cheer him up a little. I just hope no one needs a light bulb changed where we're going.

Eight Days in July
That Went Awry

Have you ever felt like you were living in the "The Twilight Zone"? I recently spent eight days there, from Sunday to Sunday.

I went to Raleigh to help my sister Nancy. She was preparing that week for her son Huck's wedding to Heather. I thought I'd calm Nancy's nerves, run errands, cook meals, and even (*so* out of character for me) clean her house. Russell, my hubby and naysayer, often says, "No good deed ever goes unpunished." He might be right.

For starters, it was hot as Hades that week. Even a supposed cool splash in our daughter Kelly's pool proved unnerving. With zillions of kids swimming around me amid *warm* water, one thing came to mind. So I jumped out, preferring to sweat off my Bain de Soleil poolside in a blasting-hot vinyl chair. That night my feet were burned. Upon inspection, they resembled bubble wrap, blistered from the scorching concrete. And I developed a cold sore the size of Cleveland above my lip.

I also watched our granddaughter, Madison, two days for Kelly. One morning we walked (but mostly sweated) around the neighborhood. The next day I drove her to My Gym for classes. Okay, I admit I was half asleep at 8 a.m.—that's early for me—when we left the house. Hours later Kelly fussed at me for sending Madison off in her pajamas. What can I say? They looked like regular clothes to me: a colorful crop top and matching capris. This Grammy Gram thing is tougher than I once thought.

Nancy and I made repeated trips to craft stores, party stores, wedding shops, and stationery shops where I clutched the coveted list that we continually added to. Once, after leaving A.C. Moore for the fourth time in two days and jumping into Nancy's car, I screamed, "The list! It's missing!" Nancy nearly slung me out of the car, turning around on two wheels while landing squarely on the sidewalk. The frightened clerk must have sensed my hysteria as she joined my buggy search, consoling me with, "Don't worry, honey." It was no use. The list was gone. I found it later inside the car, and held it tightly in my sweaty palm until bedtime.

Russell, the doubter, also says I over plan. You think? Was that because I decided we'd host my parents' sixtieth wedding anniversary celebration the same week as Huck's wedding? So what if there was a little confusion when Nancy and I simultaneously discussed entrees, cake, flowers, and slideshows—for Huck's rehearsal party, and for our parent's party. Sadly, Mom had a stomach virus and couldn't attend. We held it anyway, videoing the whole thing: twenty-eight guests toasting them.

Inside the large restaurant, Lucky 32, I managed to get lost (not so lucky). After leaving the bathroom I circled around unfamiliar faces until *finally* the manager rescued me. He placed his hand on my shoulder and guided me back to our private room, where everyone applauded. Was I really gone *that* long?

For the rehearsal dinner, I picked out a favorite dress weeks earlier. But our daughter Katie forgot to pack a dress. Flying in from a summer music festival in Sewanee, Tennessee, she had only concert-black for attire. Nancy's neighbor, Bethany Lehman, offered to lend Katie something. At the airport, I swooshed her into the bathroom and helped her quickly change into the wrap-around, mint-green linen dress with no buttons or zippers, only a sash to tie. Easy enough. She looked beautiful, though I noticed the hem lining was showing. No matter, I thought, rushing through the busy RDU airport and out to our car.

We arrived at the Cardinal Club just as the rehearsal party began. Bethany's shocked face revealed the problem, "Katie, your dress is *inside out!*" Moments later, I was the one shocked, saying to Nancy, "Did you know you have on two different black earrings?" "Oh, Ann, please tell me you are kidding," she said. "I'm not," I replied, immediately handing her my own similar black earrings. I also lent her my velvet/rhinestone flip-flops later when her achy-breaky feet started hurting. Isn't that what sisters are for?

The next day, even more wedding-related blunders surfaced.

An usher (perhaps hung over?) fouled up the seating, forcing Nancy to squeeze into an undersized pew beside Mamaw and Papaw, Giggy and Papa. That left an entire pew empty in the standing-room only church. On the next pew, Madison, one of two flower girls, was seated with us and Chuck, her daddy. Upon seeing Kelly up front, preparing to read scripture, Madison called out, "Hey, Mommy!" and waved. Everyone laughed. Otherwise, she was per-fectly quiet and well-mannered.

The air conditioning in the church wasn't cooling well. There-fore, the bride, groom, and all attendants (twenty-some in all, in tuxedoes and black and white satin gowns) were sweating bullets. I wanted to cry—from emotion, empathy, and heat.

At the lavish reception (ice carving, chocolate fondue fountain, several gourmet food stations, countless beverages) at the North Ridge Country Club, we danced till we dropped, posed for photos, and shared stories. But before the night ended, another slip up: a bridesmaid's zipper split wide open, exposing her entire back.

Huck and Heather left among cheers in a vintage Bentley for a motel an hour away, planning to fly out at 6 a.m. the following day, for Cap Jaluca, Anguilla. Nancy went home and collapsed onto the bed when the phone suddenly rang. It was Huck. "Mama, I forgot some luggage. Can you drive it over now?" Without hesitation, Nancy did so, therefore stretching the limitless theory, "that's what moms are for," to the limit.

It's no wonder I was eager to get home on the eighth day, hop-ing for some normalcy. No such luck. Our car died a mile from home, resulting in the purchase of a new alternator. I think maybe we need a new life?

Neighbors' New Mailbox Puts Us in the Doghouse

What happens when a new family moves into your neighborhood and you fail to welcome them *properly* with a gift of homemade brownies, cookies, muffins, or cake? I'll tell you one possibility. That neighbor might just ask you if you've considered replacing your rusting, dented mailbox, which is within inches of his nice, freshly painted one. That's a true story that happened to me, humorous yet embarrassing, laughable yet understandable.

One morning Russell came into the house after retrieving the newspaper (the holder is attached below our mailbox) and said our new neighbors had planted some pretty flowers in that area. Giving Russell a hard time, I asked what type of flowers, since he doesn't know the difference between a magnolia and a marigold. He said, "Oh, I don't know, daffodils or gardenias or something." I told him daffodils come from bulbs and gardenias are bushes, but he just shrugged.

Sure enough, Russell was right, as far as there being bright, lush new flowers hugging our mailbox post. I went out and inspected this newfound treasure the day after he made this announcement. There were lovely fuchsia and white petunias planted into a tight, neat circle under both mailboxes, ours and the neighbors.'

I thought to myself, "I'll bake them something and go over and thank them for such a wonderful gesture." I had already met Matt, the husband, in the driveway before the planting, but hadn't met his wife yet. But you know time flies and how busy we get?

Several weeks passed…then today I was outside and saw Matt doing yard work. He waved and I walked over to speak. After a few moments of conversation, he asked me what I thought of the mailbox area. At first I wasn't sure what he meant, having totally forgotten about the flowers. I glanced over, then covered my mouth in embarrassment. "Oh, thank you! Please forgive my manners. I forgot to say how great the flowers look." I even told him the story about Russell and his confused botanical vocabulary, which I thought was hysterical.

Matt merely nodded without too much enthusiasm and asked, "But what do you think of the *area?*" I repeated that I thought it was lovely and that the plants were blooming nicely, all the time thinking, "What else can I say about this?" I was a little dumbfounded.

I could see a perplexed look coming across Matt's face. "I mean," he started, "what about *your* mailbox? We were thinking maybe you would want to replace it."

Yikes! He was right. He hit the nail on the head. (I must add, the rust had only recently formed.) The mailbox hasn't always been an eyesore. Embarrassed, I told Matt we had noticed recently the mailbox's demise and had discussed buying a new one, just hadn't been out to do it. He even offered to get one for us. "Oh, no, but thanks," I said. He had done enough already.

Here's the thing. At one time, we had the prettiest mailbox on the street. We bought a brand new, white metal box a few years back and I sponge-painted it an attractive shade of royal blue. Then we added ceramic house numbers which were quite expensive, as I remember. Dad helped with that project, as he attached the numbers to a small, custom plaque which he painted white. Then Russell screwed the plaque onto the mailbox and finished the project by painting the post with a fresh coat of white paint.

I remember the day well. We were filled with pride and honor as we both stood back and admired our attractive new creation. Next thing we knew, another neighbor moved in and she put up a lovely new mailbox with a painted bird on it. Then, a neighbor planted a gorgeous Confederate jasmine vine. Not that I started this new trend or anything, but I did kind of pat myself on the back for bringing the neighborhood mail receptacle representation up to par. At that point, I even prided myself as the Postal Queen. Who knows? Maybe I'm the one who got everyone to hire landscape gardeners, fertilizer contractors, and lawn services? Lately it seems that everyone's yards look better than ours.

But back to the mailbox. Talk about embarrassed. Talk about

walking away with my tail between my legs. Talk about *not* calling the kettle black, but rather, calling the mailbox *trash*. I said those exact words when I called Russell at work. "Our mailbox is trash." He said he tried to warn me several weeks ago when I hit the mailbox for the forty-fifth time with my car's side view mirror, causing the forty-fifth dent on the mailbox. Hey, no one said the box has to be perfectly symmetrical, only that the mail has to be able to fit inside, and it does. Don't even bother asking me what my side view mirror looks like. Let's just say we need a can of white paint (for the mailbox) and a can of red paint (for the car).

I'm headed out of town tomorrow, but I hereby promise Matt, my other neighbors, the mailman, and the Postmaster that when I return, I will indeed replace my rickety mailbox with a brand new one. And if this doesn't end up being an all-day project, I might even find some time to bake some brownies.

Stick Around for
Mistakes, Misery, and Mystery

One day last week I got up, put the coffee on, and prepared to balance my checkbook. But when I went to pour my coffee, I saw that the decanter held no coffee—just hot water. Duh! I had forgotten to put in the filter and coffee grounds. So I poured the faked-out hot water down the drain and turned on the spigot for fresh cold water. None came out. *What's this?* I wondered, realizing my water was cut off, which never happens. Remembering that I'd seen some construction workers in my neighborhood an hour earlier, I assumed they broke the water line.

Wanting my coffee really bad but not wanting to leave the house to get a cup, I came up with a plan. I headed out to the garage, remembering I had stock-piled water earlier this summer, what with the hellacious hurricane hex that had plagued our East Coast. It took twenty full minutes to locate my water stash because I had to maneuver around bags of potting soil, golf clubs, a car, and some furniture we're trying to sell if we ever have that imaginary garage sale in the sky. (Another perfect example of procrastinating.) What is it about garages being a magnet for clutter? I always keep space open to park my car, but just beyond the perimeter is junk, which is stacked vertically, clear up to the ceiling.

I finally located the gallon jug, but couldn't tell if it was sealed. I called Russell at work to make sure he hadn't poured some weird chemical in there. He's always piddling and pouring and plodding along with something or other—cleaning his golf clubs monthly, or fertilizing our grass every ten years or so. Sometimes he has unidentified stuff left over, and I've seen him pour it in a jar or a jug. In addition to my other problems that day, I did not, repeat, did *not*, want to get poisoned.

After he verified the water's safety, I poured it through the coffee maker, with grounds in the filter, and retrieved a cup of coffee.

Then I sat down to do that most dreaded job in the world. Balance a checkbook. Not just one, but two—personal and business. Right off the bat, I noticed I had not entered the check from Piggly Wiggly the night before. So now, talk about fun, I got to sift through the trash can. Handling icky old coffee grounds from the day before, rotten banana peels, moldy bread, and something inorganic that resembled a long cottony spider web, I gave up because of those obnoxious fumes circling my head.

Next I walked out to the garage, thinking maybe the receipt was in the car. Then the phone rang and I nearly tripped on a scatter rug at the back step. It was Russell asking me if I'd seen any more, as in *additional*, lizards in the house. Did he have to remind me? Maybe that's what the shimmering, slimy object was at the bottom of the trash can. In the last week, we have found not one, but two, inside our house. As soon as Russell said that, I took off back inside the house because I believe somehow, although this has not yet been scientifically proven, that those critters are coming in through the cluttered and drafty garage. (At that point, I realized I couldn't win either way.) I prayed, "Lord, please not a lizard today, not on top of everything else."

Just then, my eyes caught sight of a small, glimmering piece of paper. I stopped to inspect it. Yes! The cash register receipt I was missing, down inside my recycled newspapers. I came back into the house, hoping against hope that I was alone (i.e., no leaping lizards).

I entered the check, ran the figures, and miraculously, was able to balance my checkbook. Feeling elated, I poured a second cup of coffee and began my search for the second checkbook register, which was nowhere to be found. That was the last straw. *Forget it*, I said, I can't take it anymore.

Looking on the bright side, it's a good thing my life is not entirely smooth—what am I saying, it's normal chaos 24/7 (an oxymoron perhaps, but nevertheless, true). But if it weren't, what would I write about? People don't want to hear about perfectionism, perkiness, and pleasantries. Instead, they seem to prefer mistakes, misery, and mystery. Don't worry, dear readers. Stick around and I'll give you plenty of all three!

Songs Sung Wrong
Almost Sound Right

I thought I was the only one who sometimes sings song lyrics wrong, but then my friend Carolyn shared this same shortcoming with me. Not only does she misspeak—or "miss sing"—but so do her daughter and a fellow employee. I wonder, *Is it us, the listeners; or is it them, the singers?* I polled a few folks and here's the results. It wasn't hard to find misconstrued lyrics—nearly everybody has one.

"Hey there, Amigo!" was Carolyn's version of "Hey, there, let me go!" from the song "Brown-Eyed Girl" by Van Morrison. Makes sense to me—hey, it is a greeting, albeit Spanish.

Marion, who works with Carolyn, said her father sang, "One ton of metal" instead of "Guantanamera," written by Jose Fernandez and sung by Pete Seeger. What do these lyrics mean anyway? A pet peeve of mine is hearing lyrics sung in a foreign language that are not later translated into English. "Voulez Vous Coucher Avec Moi, Cest Soir?" by Patti LaBelle is a good example.

How about this one that I'll call "D is for Dumb Song Lyrics Blunder?" It comes from the song "Margaritaville," sung by Jimmy Buffett. I sing, "Stepped on a Pop Tart. Blew out a flip-flop." You know that was messy! I wonder if the Pop Tart was blueberry or strawberry. The original Parrothead actually sings, "Stepped on a pop top. Blew out a flip-flop."

My daughter Katie sings, "The sky steals the limit, I'm yours," instead of "Signed, sealed, and delivered, I'm yours" from Stevie Wonder's "Signed, Sealed." I've heard of hitting a glass ceiling, but I thought the sky, in and of itself, had no limit.

Carolyn's daughter, Suzanne, sings, "Going to a party at the county fair," instead of, "Going to a party at the county jail" from Elvis Presley's "Jailhouse Rock." The title should have given her a clue that the "party" was not at a fair!

Here's a fun one: "Lay down, Sally, and rescue in my arms,"

instead of, "Lay down, Sally, and rest here in my arms." (Eric Clapton, titled, "Lay Down Sally.") Rescue in my arms? How do you "rescue" in your arms, and who or what exactly is being rescued?

I don't think we listeners ever stop to think if the lyrics we sing make sense, because let's face it, they usually don't. In fact, how often do you hear singers *stretttcchh* a word to make it rhyme? Don't even get me started on grammar. I can hear the entire recording industry shouting, "It's not about the grammar!" Oh yes it is! At least that's what Lynne Truss might say, author of the *New York Times* best-selling book, *Eats, Shoots and Leaves.* She might even title a sequel *Songs Sung Wrong.* Or is that "Song Sung Blue" by Neil Diamond?

Okay, here's some more. How about, "Give me the Beach Boys and free my soul. I want to get lost in your rock and roll." The right version is, "Give me the beat, boys, and free my soul." Living like I do at the beach, that word "beach" does come up often, so that's an honest mistake. That song is by Dobie Gray and titled, "Drift Away."

Another friend, Marilyn, said her son used to sing "Shaving!" instead of "Shameless!" (also the song's title) by Garth Brooks. Those words just might work for a Gillette commercial.

Remember "Kind of a Drag?" by The Buckinghams? A lady I know says her son sang, "Canada Dry!" Another commercial!

And finally, here's a new take on an old song by Elton John: "Hold me closer, Tony Danza!" instead of "Hold me closer, tiny dancer." The song is titled, "Tiny Dancer." I won't even comment on that one.

Sometimes I sing the lyrics wrong to church hymns, but that has nothing to do with not understanding the words. It's because I can't read the small print in the hymnals. To make matters worse, Russell and I have the exact opposite vision: He is far-sighted and I am near-sighted. When we share the hymnal, which we've learned not to unless forced, our bodies sway like palm trees in a tropical breeze, going back and forth.

Well, today is Katie's twentieth birthday and I think I've got these lyrics right. Let me see here, oh yeah. "Happy birthday to you! Happy birthday to you! Happy birthday, dear Katie, happy birthday to you. And many more!" (How'd I do?)

I Found a Fork in the Road and Took It—No, Really!

I once wrote a column titled "My Dad's Gone Psychic." Well, y'all, Dad's done it again. Gone psychic. Predicting the future. This is getting spooky. A couple of weeks ago Dad and I were talking on the phone. I was asking his advice about a tough decision I was facing. I have tremendous respect for my dad. He has proven over and over that life is what you make it. For instance, he began working in a shoe store at age seventeen, quickly became the manager, and eventually bought the store from his boss. At one time, he owned three shoe stores, but is now "actively retired." By that, I mean he's busier as a retiree than he ever was while working. He is now golfing, traveling, woodworking, and serving as landlord to a small shopping center that he owns. Dad works circles around me. And did I mention that he's frugal? He probably has the first dollar he ever earned.

As we talked about this dilemma I was facing, Dad said he was reminded of a quote. I thought, *Ah, this will be profound. He's going to make a strong point to get his message across.* But instead he said, "If you come to a fork in the road, take it!" Hmmmm…I'd heard that expression before. It made no sense then and it made no sense now. Perplexed, I said, "Oh, well, okay," wondering if it was just me that didn't get it.

I later told this story to Russell who memorizes famous quotes. "Oh yeah," he said. "Yogi Berra said that. It makes no sense; most of his quotes don't." "Exactly," I replied. Russell continued, "Here's a couple more quotes by him that also make no sense. 'Why buy good luggage? You only use it when you travel,' and, 'Baseball is 90% mental—the other half is physical.'"

I didn't give the fork quote much thought until a week later when Russell and I were visiting my parents in North Carolina. As we often do, Russell and I went for a brisk, long walk through their neighborhood. We ended up in the high school parking lot and were about to take a sharp left, when I saw this shiny object lying in the road. I am not making this up. To my astonishment, it was a fork! Not a spoon, or a knife, or even a bracelet (which you sometimes find), but an honest to goodness *fork*. In fact, it was as flat as a pancake, as if cars had driven over it several times. I nearly gave Russell a heart attack when I jumped to grab it. I hurried home to show Dad my treasure. I said, "I came to a fork in the road, and I took it! Now what?"—hoping that finally, the mystery would be solved. However, Dad was speechless and I'm still clueless.

Funny things can show up in life, and I guess that fork is my most unusual find. Of course, my lost diamond ring was my favorite find. But the most puzzling find was when Russell and I returned from a vacation and found a red wheelbarrow propped up on the side of our house. (Ten years later, it's still a mystery.) One lost item I never saw again was sunglasses I forgot at the post office. An employee, Terri, told me I'd left a pair, but when she went to retrieve them from the lost and found box, they were gone—lost again!

The most disappointing item I've ever lost, and still not found, was a sterling silver anklet that Russell bought me in St. Marten. The weirdest thing I've ever "lost" (that wasn't truly lost) was when I left behind a couple of pounds of boiled peanuts in a refrigerator at a posh hotel in Wrightsville Beach, North Carolina. I was speaking at a seminar and meant to deliver them to the event planner, in appreciation, but forgot. When I came home, I remembered them and called the hotel and explained this to the receptionist. She said, "Hold on. I'll transfer you to lost and found." I told her, no, that wasn't necessary, since they were perishable. If they were found, surely they were either eaten or thrown away. Ignoring that, she said, "Tell me something. I've never eaten boiled peanuts." (Obviously, she was not from around here!) She continued, "Don't they taste like beans?" Hard to believe I was having this conversation. Sounds like something I would ask.

Well, before I lose my train of thought (which happens several times per hour), I believe I'll end this column. Anyway, I'm at a loss of words. I hope your losses are few and your gains are great.

Later, I Found a Fork and a Job (But Only Kept One)

Many folks were intrigued by my column, "I Found a Fork in the Road and Took It—No, Really!" A lady asked me to share a dilemma I mentioned in another column: I was offered a job and took it (think of the fork as a metaphor); but unlike the actual fork, which I kept, I didn't keep the job. I worked eight hours and "lost it." In other words, I resigned—fork or no fork!

It all began when my best friend called me and said a boutique owner was looking for part-time help. My friend said, "Ann, you would be perfect! Just look at all the things you've sold over the years: shoes, telephone systems, books." It was true that I'd had relatively good success at selling, so I gave the boutique owner a call.

She invited me in for an interview and hired me right then and there. The job sounded exciting, interesting, and rewarding. Another perk: I'd get out of the house a few days each week and pick up some extra cash.

I wish I could tell you that everything went well. Actually, it did (the first day, that is). The following day didn't. I woke up with an aching back, a headache, and swollen feet. This part-time job ended up being just that. I parted in no time.

Standing for nearly eight hours was killer because I wasn't used to it. And this is coming from someone in fairly good physical shape: I'm a speed walker and I stay busy cooking, gardening, or piddling around. But this was different.

In addition, as they say, "retail ain't what it used to be." There were so many things to remember: straightening the racks, tags facing forward, grouping similar styles, colors, and brands. Ringing up sales on a computer (nothing like the old days where you simply punched in a price, like $49.50). It's not like I don't know my way around a keyboard, either. Microsoft Word is second nature to me. I can even type 100 words per minute, for goodness' sake. But this involved typing stock numbers, code words, and verifying prices; choosing the method of pay; and all the while, smiling, counting back change, neatly folding the garments in a nice, crisp paper bag with a foil logo, tying multi-colored ribbons around the handle, and then (whew!) remembering to write down exactly what was sold for restocking later. Ditto for jewelry and shoes. And if another customer walked in just then—well, forget about remembering anything. It was too much!

All of these duties were making me dizzy and I guess it showed. At 1:45 the boss asked me if I was okay. That's exactly what she said. "Are you okay?" She mentioned that my eyes had a glazed-over look.

I didn't even try to hide the fact. "Well, actually, I'm hungry!" I whined, sounding like a kindergartner. Working from home (writing full-time now and medical transcribing previously for twelve years), I ate when I was hungry, having the freedom to do so. I knew my hypoglycemia was kicking in because my hands were shaking. Though the boss had said on the interview that I could take a lunch hour (by giving some notice), I brought lunch from home that day. That is, if you can call it lunch.

Since I didn't know if a refrigerator existed (turns out it did), I brought a plain old peanut butter and jelly sandwich, an orange, and a few pretzels. I also threw in a boring bottle of water—not even my usual tea-caffeine fix, and obviously not my typical girlfriends' lunch out. Admittedly, the crowded dimly-lit stock room was used mainly for inventory, so I sat on a metal folding stool, scrunched up to a merchandising cart. Within moments, I began to dream about a vacation! And that wasn't even an option because no benefits were offered. By late afternoon, I feared the next day.

Later, at home, I felt weary, teary, and not so cheery. My sweet and understanding hubby agreed there was only one thing to do. Go in and give a notice. But how much notice, I wondered? An hour for every day I worked? What was the precedent here? We both agreed it was unfair to let the boss spend time and energy training me, then count on me when my body was screaming, "Help!" At a certain age, you *learn* to listen to your body 'cause if you don't, it has ways of making you wish you did! This job was just not meant to be.

Luckily, the boss was very kind. I arrived on time the next day. Before I could say "untrainable," she was training me once again—starting fresh at the computer and counting out the money. I bit my lower lip and finally broke in, saying, "We need to talk." She guessed it. "You can't do this, can you?" I smiled weakly, explaining my bad back. She didn't seem surprised. I guess she saw me limping to my car the night before. We decided I'd finish out the morning and call it a day—and a job, for that matter. I thanked her for her sincerity and compassion. Then I left the boutique and had a *real* lunch with my best friend, who promised not to recommend any other jobs.

It's true that I wound up with three chic outfits, comfortable and trendy. However, I only earned enough to pay for one—and *that* was with my employee discount. So much for that vacation I was dreaming about!

The Name Game Is One I Can't Remember How to Play

Would'a, should'a, could'a, didn't. When it comes to people's names, how many times have I wished I would'a, should'a, could'a remembered theirs—but didn't? That's especially true with someone I'm meeting for the first time. I tried that Dale Carnegie seminar tip where they train you to remember names using word association. That didn't work either. I met "Inca" at the gym, and associating her name with the ancient ruins in Mexico, I then called her "Maya."

Maybe I was jinxed years ago when I made the mistake of naming both daughters with the same beginning K consonant: Kelly and Katie. Most times, either name comes out as a blend of the two, Kayley or Keddie. The writer in me who loves alliteration couldn't resist. But let me warn you, don't do that to your children because the Christmas card-signing cuteness wears off fast. And another thing—every time Kelly visits here from Raleigh, I call Katie "Kelly" for the next two weeks. Must be a mama thing.

My dad had a similar problem forty-some years ago when naming my brother Steve. Dad's brother's name is Cecil. More often than not, Steve is called "Stecil." And to make matters worse, Cecil is called also "Stecil"!

But wait. There's more. My nephew's name is Huck Huxley (try saying that three times fast). My son-in-law's name is Chuck. They live one mile apart in Raleigh. Obviously, I often see them both on trips to North Carolina. Together these guys are often mislabeled as "Huck/Chuck" and it comes out like "Up-chuck." Ick! I mean, uck! And my family's crazy rhyming names don't end there. Steve's wife's name is Lori, and they named their son Cory. I'm beginning to feel like we're living in a Dr. Seuss book.

Argghhh. You can see how these brothers' and sisters', nieces' and nephews' names can become tongue twisters. But how do you explain calling your husband or wife by the wrong name? Hmmm. I still find it hard to believe that this happened, but darn it, there was a witness, so I can't deny it. Once, when Russell, Kelly, and I were eating out, both said I called Russell "Roger." I still think this tale was a plot to drive me crazy, and evidently it worked…because here I am many years later, no saner now than I was then. (One possible reason for this mistaken identity was that I once had a boss named Roger, but it was many moons ago and there was no resemblance between him and Russell. For one thing, Russell doesn't hand me a paycheck every two weeks, and for another, I don't balance his books. Write books, yes. *Balance* books? Rarely!)

I want so much to remember people's names, and I appreciate it when someone does the same for me. I think it's simply good manners to speak a person's name when talking with them, and to make eye contact, too. But it's hard to say a name when you can't remember it—and you're better off saying nothing than saying it wrong.

Case in point: A few years back, a banker came to our house for us to sign a note for a car. He was our neighbor and we knew each other casually because our children were in Waccamaw High School together. He arrived at our house, opened his briefcase, and began explaining the fine details of the contract—annual percentage rate, payment amount, length of the loan, and so forth.

Practicing those good manners I just mentioned, I made good eye contact and spoke his name—Michael—frequently. I even offered Michael a glass of sweet tea with lemon. What kind of a Southern hostess would I be if I hadn't? Later, after the business dealings were over, I asked Michael which street he lived on, and he pointed one street over. Then we discussed the school's marching band. The more we talked, the more I liked Michael. He was interesting, witty, and personable.

When he stood to leave, he shook Russell's and my hand, then reached into a pocket, and handed us each a business card. I thanked him, briefly looked at the card, and then froze in embarrassment. I said, "Jerome? Who's Jerome?" "Me," he said, rather shyly, looking down. "Well, then…." I started. "Who's Michael?" He shrugged his shoulders. "Why did you let me call you that all evening? Oh, I am so embarrassed," I told him. (Russell was late for the appointment, so he wasn't there when Jerome first arrived.) The two of them broke out into hysterical laughter as I stood there and silently repeated "Jerome" a dozen times to myself.

Another name folly: One time, Russell and I were greeters at church. When a lady stepped forward, Russell said, "Hello, Dorothy. Nice to see you." Thinking she was the Dorothy that I knew—the mother of Bert (a Sunday school friend)—I quickly responded. "Hi, Dorothy. How is Bert?" She raised her eyebrow, stepped back, and asked, "Who is Bert?" Sorry, wrong Dorothy.

All this difficult name remembering reminds me of a game (and one I always lose). You could call it *The Name Game*. Remember the popular song of the same name from years ago? We heard it playing the other night at a nearby restaurant, where Katie is waitressing this summer before returning to the University of South Carolina. That night, Katie was sitting with us at our table dining, since she had worked the earlier shift. When we started hearing, "Marsha, Marsha, Mo Marsha, Banana Bana, Bo Barsha, Fe, Fi, Fo, Marsha. *Marsha!*" Katie covered her ears and started screaming, "I hate that song!" Well, she got it honest. I rolled my eyes and replied, "Oh, Kayley. It's not that bad." Roger agreed.

CHAPTER 4
Food Fit for Foodies
and Kitchen Capers

Sushi in the South

I realize the subject of sushi is old news (along with tape decks and hair perms) and yet, I've just become a fan. When I first tried sushi over eight years ago, I didn't see what the big deal was. At that time, a friend who frequently stopped at a certain Japanese steakhouse took me along. I wasn't too excited, frankly: a little fish, a little seaweed, a little rice. But you know what the best part was to me, then and now? The condiments. The pickled ginger and wasabi. (I guess these would be considered condiments?)

Sushi does have redeemable qualities. It's hard to argue about the health benefits—highly nutritious and low-calorie. That's probably why we seldom see fat Asian sushi chefs. They're usually lean, trim, and though I don't know why, blessed with lots of dark, thick hair. Hey, maybe some of our "healthy" Southern friends need to go on a sushi diet (no names, please).

Bess, a dear friend, has started a sushi girls' dining experience and we meet every other Tuesday for wine, sushi, and stimulating conversation. At our group's first gathering, I proved you can't take the country out of the girl. For starters we were served some crackle bread with dip and a bowl of edamame (which tastes similar to boiled peanuts). I've read about these green, succulent soy beans, but I'm a Southern girl, after all. Put a bowl of beans in front of me and I assume they're ready for immediate consumption. Plus, they look similar to sugar snap peas and snow pea pods which are eaten whole. I picked up a "bean"—the entire outer pod, that is—and plopped it into my mouth. Ick! It turned out to be a tough and fibrous, stringy mess, which yes, should have been shelled first. Desperate to spit it out, I had no choice but to cough into my white cloth napkin. The waiter caught sight of this, and in horror, dashed to our table to see if everything was all right. "Well, no," I garbled, motioning for a new napkin. He probably imagined this redneck mama wouldn't leave a tip. Ha! I fooled him. I may be uninformed, but I do tip well.

I have one question about sushi. How do you eat it with chopsticks? I mean, how in the world are you supposed to grasp that one-and-a-half-inch roll of sushi with those awkward, hard-to-handle chopsticks that only open one inch? You can't cut the roll in half with a knife because A) the restaurant doesn't give you one; and B) even if they did, you *cannot* cut through that shiny, black, elastic-like seaweed coating. Why must life be so complicated?

On a recent trip out of town I bought some sushi to go, simply for the practice of using chopsticks. Sitting there alone, I put a rubber band around the sticks like they do for kids in restaurants. It was no use. The sticks went flying and the sushi went rolling!

One last note. What's up with that green seaweed salad? It does not seem like an edible form of food. It's one thing to be swirling around in the ocean, surrounded by jelly fish, man o'war, and other flotilla. But as open-minded as I am and as adventurous as I can be, I can't seem to distinguish the eerie taste. It's not quite salty, but it is slimy. It's rubbery, and it's chewy. Oh heck, it's just plain gross.

Well, folks, we've made some real inroads here in the South when it comes to sushi. This was proven to me recently when several of us attended a dinner party and everyone was asked to bring their favorite dish (homemade or store-bought). My best friend, Carolyn, didn't bring fried chicken, deviled eggs, or potato salad—mainstays in the Deep South. Honey, she brought sushi! For real.

The sushi girls are meeting again next week. I'll try to remember to get everything straight before I attend: pop the edamame, get a grip on the chopsticks, and skip the seaweed salad. Oh yeah, and most important—have a good time!

TV Host's Biggest Blooper: Flaming Pantyhose

With permission from Diane DeVaughn Stokes, my friend and the popular TV host of "Southern Style" and owner of Stages Video, I'm going to tell a few of her best stories, using Diane's words:

One time a man walked into Stages Video to sell video tapes. He was just absolutely full of himself. He took one look at me and said, "I need to speak to someone who can make a decision around here." I cleared my throat, saying "You got her." "No, no, no. Not you!" he said. "I mean, like, an officer in the company." I answered, "I *am* an officer. Can I help you?" He continued, "Oh, you're the secretary? No, I'm not talking about the secretary."

At this point I was fuming. I quickly informed him, "Okay, three strikes and you're out. First, I *am* the president here. Second, let this be a lesson: I'm not even going to speak to you. Just because a woman is involved in a business doesn't mean she isn't influential. And third, never minimize the secretary because that person often makes the decisions." He apologized profusely, saying, "Let's start over." But I would have no part of that and I sent him on his way.

My husband, Chuck, likes to say about me, "Tick her off once and it's okay. Tick her off twice and it's still okay. But *don't* tick her off a third time! Otherwise, Diane is the easiest going person in the world."

Many years ago I was doing a show in Florence called "Live: Pee Dee People" (named after the Pee Dee River in South Carolina) on Channel 15. The guest I was interviewing, unfortunately, had his zipper undone the entire time. It was difficult not to be distracted with his underwear showing through. But we were televising live, so I couldn't tell him. Sometimes guests break out in hives from a case of "nerves." I didn't have hives, but I know my face was red that day!

Another day, a woman's wig fell off. She was on my TV show dressed as a litter person. She was called Litter Flitter. She went around the schools promoting an anti-litter campaign. She even had a "litter wand" with a star on the end of it. She went to shake her little fairy wand when a point in the star got caught in her wig, jerking it off her head, showing only her stocking cap. "Oh, my God," she gasped. "My husband is going to kill me!"

While taping a show one day, the lights suddenly went out. I discovered later it was because someone had hit a telephone pole. We finished the show in the dark amid my repeated questioning. But the director said, "Keep talking." "How?" I said, "We've got no lights." "Keep talking!" he demanded. None of this, of course, was taped. Not the interview or the director's demands.

One day a sushi chef named Saito caught my pantyhose on fire. His claim to fame was to debone a chicken in less than one minute, then cook it in teriyaki. He could not speak English. He could only manage to say, "No speak English." I couldn't believe the owner of the restaurant sent a chef that could not speak English. Like, I would do the talking and the chef would do the cooking during the interview?

Chef Saito turned on the hibachi and a spark went off, landing on my leg. I grabbed the dishrag off the table, banging it on my leg. Suddenly, the chef said, "Oh no! We have to start over." I looked at him. "You said you couldn't speak English!" He answered, "I lied." After that, I told everyone, "I may love my husband, Chuck, but Saito is the only one to set my pantyhose on fire!"

Secret Recipes
Have No Place in My Kitchen

One of my favorite hobbies is cooking. That is, when the conditions are right: If I have a decent sized group dining at the house (it's hard to get excited over cooking for two), and if someone volunteers to clean up afterwards. During those times you'll find me at the stove—slicing, stirring, and smiling. Call me Betty Crocker. Um, make that Ina Garten, my fave Food TV guru and host of "Barefoot Contessa." Ina is such a sincere soul with a warm-hearted laugh, who couldn't love her?

I especially enjoy my time in the kitchen during the holidays, except for Thanksgiving. I almost always succumb to my "Thanksgiving Hex." In the past, I've caught the oven on fire, nearly served undercooked Cornish hens, found buffet selections in restaurants scarce and tasteless, and cooked a turkey on a new smoker, only to have the bird taste like the hickory chips that topped the charcoal.

Being in a supper club, coupled with having gourmet friends, part of our culinary interests involves sharing recipes. We all do it; we've all done it; we'll all continue to do it. But evidently, some don't. My friend Becky told me she'd met someone who didn't give out recipes. I was appalled. I mean, that is so not right. Isn't that a little outdated, and dare I say, selfish? I asked Becky to tell me more.

It seems that the woman in question, upon hearing compliments on her dish, perked up. She shook her head, and therefore, her blonde, flipped hairdo, from side to side, giggled nervously, and with a way-too-wide smile, in a charming voice, said, "Why, thank you, y'all!" batting her eyelashes. But things suddenly changed for the worst when someone asked her for the recipe. She turned into a monster. Although putrid smoke didn't exactly pour out of her mouth, Becky said her nostrils did flare a bit. The woman then barked out her refusal, "Oh no, I don't, I don't." Her shocked audience gasped; their mouths dropped open. Then the transformed half-woman, half-witch with the secret drew in a deep breath as her eyes narrowed. She held her head high, and with pointed finger and forked tongue announced, "I don't give out my recipes. You see, they are *family secrets*." Yeah, well, so are lots of other unmentionables, but eventually someone squeals, thereby making front-page headlines— or at the very least, creating juicy gossip. That creature was lucky the group didn't seize her and burn her at the stake.

I mean, you just don't *not* give out recipes. It's part of an unwritten etiquette rule. Besides, that's the highest compliment a cook can receive. Heck, not only do I want to give out the recipe, I can't wait to taste it when it's done. That way, I get a night off from cooking. That, plus I want to see if theirs is better than mine, a theory akin to, "Food is always better when you don't have to cook it yourself."

I once overheard a woman in a restaurant who didn't get this. She said, "Sally, I'm ordering the crab quiche because I want to see if it's as good as mine." And y'all, you just *know* it was. It was all I could do not to jump up and scream, "Woman, are you crazy? This is a four-star restaurant in one of the oldest and finest cities in South Carolina, namely Charleston, sitting on a street named after an aristocratic Southern family. Of course it will be better than yours!" Women (including me) can be chatty, but we can also be catty.

I love the restaurants that give out their recipes. That's one reason I've subscribed to *Bon Appetit* all these years. I love to collect and prepare recipes. Recently, I decided to try out a recipe provided by a trendy local restaurant. To tell you the truth, it sounded a little bland to begin with, calling for only a few simple ingredients. No truffle oil, no saffron, no strange food that you find only in an obscure specialty market. Forging ahead, I cooked it *exactly* as the recipe instructed. We sat down to eat and I was the first to say, "This dish doesn't have much flavor. Maybe it needs some Worcestershire sauce, thyme, dry mustard…" Sadly, no one disagreed.

I also questioned if an ingredient was missing, either by mistake, or on purpose. You never know. What I do know is that I wrote on the card, "Consider spicing this up—or else, consider throwing this recipe out!" One thing's for sure, I'll gladly share it with you if you ask.

"Gerbil Food"
Leaves Me Hungry

Well, dang. It happened again. I went out to dinner, then came home hungry. This was after dining in a posh restaurant with tuxedoed waiters and a superb waterfront view.

Tonight I had dinner with a dear friend Ronda Rich, author of *What Southern Women Know About Flirting* who is herself a classy Southern diva. Ronda even coined the phrase, "Dixie Divas." Don't you love it? Now that's a group I want to join. In her column entitled "Dixie Divas," she recently wrote, "We must uphold and preserve all things dear to southern womanhood we love so…A Dixie Diva personifies all that southern women hold dear—grace, charm, compassion, humor, tenacity, home, and family…"

But back to dinner. I ordered a lobster appetizer and a side salad. It wasn't that I was trying to cut corners. In fact, I actually ended up spending equal to or more than the average entrée. Ronda ordered a lobster entrée. Her meal came with a salad. After dinner we chatted about everything from writing to careers to family.

I was so engrossed in the conversation that I didn't realize I was still hungry after the server took my plate away. (But I can promise you that I ate everything on it!) Once I got home, my stomach started growling. Not a muffled rumble, but a really loud "Grrrrr, feed me something *now!*"

Why is it that the fancier the restaurant and the higher the menu prices, the less the food volume? I've noticed more and more in those upscale eateries chock-full of trendy furnishings, uniformed wait staff, breath-taking views, and savvy-looking patrons that a garden salad consists of perhaps three lettuce leaves, chopped into ribbons (which falls off the fork), two cucumber slices cut nicely on the diagonal, four cherry tomatoes, and a sliver of purple onion. Come on y'all, that's not dinner. That's gerbil food. The salad wasn't the only thing eye-catching (and small) that night. The entrée was a kaleidoscope of color, what with those fancy swirls of orange, red, and green sauce. Do they really think all that beautification will satisfy you even though there is no real food quantity on the plate? When the waiter asked, "Would you ladies like some dessert?" I should have replied, "Sure, at some point, but actually, Antonio, first I think I need another meal to fill me up."

Well, I came home and did what any normal, healthy, starving woman would've done. I fixed me a snack. A big snack. This consisted of a half bag of popcorn, a half dozen Hershey Kisses, and a dozen cashews—my own version of poppycock. I let that settle, but felt hungry an hour later. I ate a fruit snack-pack. Still hungry, I drank a big glass of milk, since that was easier than preparing real food (although a PB&J was sounding good about now).

Considering I've been dubbed a fast food snob by my family and friends (who, by the way, aren't lying), I am thinking seriously of converting. I mean at least with a Big Fat Meat 'n Unknown Filler Greaseburger, you do get full. Right? And let's just double up that Mega-Quantum, So Salty You'll be Thirsty All Day French Fries with a Super Thick (Forget Using a Straw) Chocolate Shake. No one promised this mammoth meal would be low calorie, but at least I'd be spared the trouble of fixing another meal within an hour.

And to think, all week—okay I'm lying, all month—I've been thinking about starting a new food plan, but not a diet. I can't even stand the word "diet," which by the way stands for, "Did I Eat That?" because you are never sure. You're so busy buying the food, coming home and unloading, washing, sorting, measuring and re-reading the daggumed diet book, that you can't remember if you ate or not.

Hey, if I keep eating at those fancy restaurants, I'll lose weight because they'll unwittingly put me on a diet, with no complicated food planning on my part. I'll just show up every night at one of those places with the two and three digit menu prices.

Russell says he is not surprised by this "I'm starving" dilemma because he distinctly remembers on our first date that I ate more than he did. I'll never forget it. We were in the very finest restaurant in my small hometown, a rustic log cabin on the outskirts of town that used tablecloths, linen napkins, and candles on the table. They stood out among the other spots because they didn't have "diner," "café," or "truck stop" on the carved-wood sign out front. It quickly became the hot spot.

At the end of our romantic evening, Russell opened the door for us to leave. *Aha, a gentleman,* I thought. The next part I'll never forget.

He said, "Ann, I want to you tell you something. I can't—"

"Yes?" I accidentally interrupted, thinking he was going to give me a huge compliment, like, "I can't believe how shiny your hair is," or "I can't believe how much fun you are." Yeah, right.

Instead, he said, "I can't believe how much you can eat." True story. You see, where Russell comes from (rural Jones County, North Carolina), with all those husky, strong farm girls, he thought he was giving me a compliment. Oh well, some things never change. Here we are twenty-four years later, and I'm still hungry. I'd better sneak in that PB&J lest he *commend* me again tonight.

Southern Traditions: Boiled Peanuts and Blueberry Cobbler

Have you ever noticed how we Southerners are big on traditions, and that these traditions usually revolve around food? Even though nowadays few of us have time to till the soil, sow the seeds, and cultivate a half-acre garden, many of us remember a time when our parents, grandparents, or neighbors did. And even in the hurried twenty-first century, some of us still find time to cook these comfort foods—or at the very least, order them at one of the local Mom & Pop restaurants.

My personal favorite summertime food is boiled peanuts, pronounced *bald* peanuts by us diehard Southerners. The very thought of them brings back warm memories, as is often the case with food. How they are prepared (and eaten) is quite unique. I know of no other food you must boil in heavily salted water for three hours, then work like the dickens to open. They're a little like steamed oysters: a lot of work for a small reward, but downright irresistible.

I believe we were in the sixth grade when my best friend, Jenny Demary, brought out a colander full of boiled peanuts one July night and we sat on her front porch stoop, watching fireflies and swatting mosquitoes, talking about cute boys and cheerleading practice. Her father was a dentist and a patient had brought him this heavenly snack—and Jenny was the coolest girl in school. She lived in a comfortable, country estate-type home, had a large, close-knit family, and a full-time maid. I was in awe of her.

Jenny was also a rebel. She showed me how to shave my legs, much to my mother's chagrin—and she taught me how to iron. She lent me her Villager sweaters and experimented with my hair, putting it up or curling it into a flip. But my favorite memories of Jenny and me, to this day, were eating those boiled peanuts—smelling the briny aroma, popping them open, giggling as juice ran down our elbows, moaning when the flavor hit our taste buds, and then tossing the empty shells to the ground.

Since then I've probably cooked or consumed a hundred pounds of boiled peanuts...but I have noticed this tradition is mainly a Southern thing. I've tried to convert a few friends who aren't from here, but they turn up their noses.

While it's true boiled peanuts can be a little problematic—sometimes they are hard to open with your fingers and you must resort to using your teeth—these goobers are well worth the trouble. The exception is when you get a bad one and there is no peanut inside, but trashy, fibrous, brown gunk instead. Another problem is their short shelf life. If you accidentally leave them out on the kitchen counter for three or four days, they become slimy and smelly and someone (probably you) will say, "What in the heck stinks?"

I was thrilled recently to see a huge bowl of boiled peanuts in the buffet line at a local restaurant—a new, family-owned, upscale yet reasonably priced establishment that serves home-cooked food. Sitting among the fried chicken, macaroni and cheese, sautéed okra, and peach cobbler, there they were! Those kidney-shaped, mottled-looking, homely brown shells. They are a true representation of the quote, "It's what's inside that counts." Why, boiled peanuts have even replaced my former homemade gift du jour, those gooey, death-by-chocolate brownies I was once famous for.

Other foods signal meaningful traditions too. In the Morris family (my maiden name), when blueberry and peach season rolls around, my sisters and I cook delicious cobblers like our late, great Granny Pinky often made. (I'll share her recipe at the end of this column.) The best part is you can make it in a black iron skillet, tie a bandanna around the handle (when it's cooled), and serve it to your family, supper club, or church social. It's a real show-stopper with the culinary crowd.

We had many Morris traditions: canning string beans, tomatoes, and chow-chow, the latter being a pickle-relish that is superb on hot dogs or mixed in cole slaw. In most homes, all of this canning or "putting up," the old Southern term, was traditionally done by women. So imagine my shock when I called my Dad recently and he told me he was *cooking* and *canning* boiled peanuts. I nearly dropped the phone. As a kid, I never saw my Dad actually cook anything. He only wandered into the kitchen during mealtime. He told me a friend of his explained the technique and ingredients needed to master this feat, and the next thing he knew, he'd put up some eight quarts himself.

Since Dad is doing the peanut thing, I'll bring him and Mom a different gift of food next week when I visit: Granny Pinky's blueberry cobbler.

GRANNY PINKY'S "5-IN-1" ALL-TIME BEST-EVER COBBLER

1 stick of butter
1 cup of self-rising flour
1 cup of sugar
1 cup of milk, whole or evaporated
1–2 cups of fruit (blueberries or peaches)

Melt the butter in a 350-degree oven in a cast iron skillet. Mix the other four ingredients in a separate bowl and pour atop the butter. *Do not mix* once it hits the pan. Cook at 350 degrees for about 45 minutes or until it's golden bubbly.
Enjoy!

"Not a Problem," Said the Waiter, as He Grabbed the Chatty Wife

Sundays are a special day for me. I happen to believe that the good Lord intended for us to rest on the Sabbath, and so I try. I realize that "rest" is open to interpretation. For me, a typical Sunday means enjoying one of our minister's dynamic sermons. This is followed by lunch, where Russell and I discuss the morning's sermon at one of our favorite restaurants, enjoy a relaxing meal, and plan the up-coming week. After that, we head home and the day is up for grabs. Sometimes we piddle around in the yard. Other times Russell hits range balls and I buy groceries. If I'm hearing the muse, I might write a column. Occasionally, we go see a matinee. But the real fun usually occurs at lunch.

If you're people-watchers like we are, you know exactly what I mean. There are lots of places to observe (okay, I'll tell it like it is, *to eavesdrop on*) the human race, but my favorite spot is in restaurants. However, I'm beginning to worry. Maybe Russell and I have been studying the masses too seriously lately because *everyone* is starting to remind us of *someone*.

For example, last night we went to a lovely wedding, followed by a fabulous, high-falluting reception under a big white tent—big-time doings for our small town. We feasted on planks of grilled salmon, shrimp and grits, pulled pork, a smorgasbord cheese tray, fruit fondue with a scrumptious chocolate, to-die-for wedding cake, and so forth and so on, and then we listened to a great band. We had a blast! Everyone I saw thoroughly enjoyed themselves.

While having lunch out today, Russell said one of the hostesses looked just like the bride from the recent wedding, though I know the bride and groom were long gone on their honeymoon. We even recited our private joke where one of us says, "That man reminds me of Tom Cruise." And the other person says, "*Everybody* reminds you of *somebody*."

While dining out, I pay close attention to the wait staff. They are some of the most interesting people. But have you noticed that one annoying habit? The catch phrase they all say—"Not a problem"—to *everything*. My simple request might be, "May I have some ketchup, please?" I'm told, "Not a problem." If I get more demanding with, "Could you turn down that blaring music?" Again they smile and say, "Not a problem." It's like they're cheerful robots, programmed to say that perfect, short sentence. I'm tempted to test them, you know, try to mess them up with, "I come here a lot and y'all have never offered me a frequent diner card like your competition next door. So how 'bout if you just trust me when I say I've eaten here ten times in the past two months. Wouldn't that make this meal, my eleventh, a freebie?" Do you think they'd do it, or would they say, "*Is* a problem"?

While eating out today, we saw several of our church friends. I ran into my dear friend Nancy Rhyne, one prolific author, who wrote *Low Country Voices* and nineteen other books. I saw Nancy come in with her husband, Sid, but didn't get to speak to them immediately because they were waiting for a table. When they did get seated about ten minutes later, they sat one booth over from us. Instinctively, I hopped up to speak to them, leaving Russell behind. I overheard him mumbling, "Well, I knew that was going to happen." Nancy and I have so much in common and both love to chat, and since I hadn't really sat down and talked to her in months, the time flew by. What fun to be in the company of Nancy and Sid. We were discussing books, publishing, and tour schedules.

That conversation led to talking about the admirable art of navigating the highways and Nancy inquired about Russell's navigational skills. Now if you've read my column much during the past four and half years, you know that neither Russell nor I can follow a road map. Nancy admitted to getting lost in Greenville one time. But she told me that Sid is quite the road wizard. He then promised to help us find our next destination. Forget MapQuest, Sid's directions are much more user-friendly, according to Nancy.

During the middle of our conversation, Ryan, our waiter, walked over to get their drink order. I told him just to ignore me, I was booth-hopping, and he said he thought I looked familiar.

While chatting non-stop, I noticed out of the corner of my eye that our meal had arrived, but I didn't want to stop talking to eat. I know, I know. That doesn't sound like me, but it's true. I heard Russell clear his throat and watched him give me *the look*. Then I saw him shrug his shoulders, take a deep breath, pick up his fork, and dig right in. Next I saw Russell and Ryan engrossed in a heavy conversation, both staring holes through me. Uh oh. I stood up to tell Nancy and Sid goodbye at the same time Ryan appeared with a sheepish smile.

When I sat down across from Russell, he said, "I thought I was going to have to eat my entire meal alone." I patted him on the hand and said, "Oh honey, I'm so sorry. I saw that our meal had come, but I was just having such a wonderful time catching up with Nancy."

Now I know why Ryan had that smile on his face. Russell told me that Ryan asked him when his meal was nearly over, "Sir, is everything okay? Can I get you anything else?" Russell, in his off-handed, sarcastic way answered, "Yes, my wife." And you know what Ryan said? *"Not a problem!"*

Lobsters and Collards, the Poor Things!

I heard an expression the other day that's rarely said anymore: *the poor thing*. It's loosely the equivalent of the Southern adage, *bless her heart*.

But "the poor thing" carries a heavier weight. It implies pity, sympathy, and—heaven forbid—sometimes, even jealousy. It's true that pious Southern women don't like to admit to the sins of envying, coveting, and jealousy—but heck, Southern women don't like to admit to any sins. However, like Aunt Bee on "The Andy Griffith Show," who once made a mistake by opening a Chinese restaurant, we aren't perfect either.

In order to fully understand the expression "the poor thing," we need to know a little background information. An example is women gossiping in the beauty parlor (the third most popular activity there, right behind getting your roots tipped and your mustache dipped). One woman says, "Wanda, the poor thing, she must feel foolish driving that gas-guzzling monster truck while her husband, Ned, is in the Big House."

See? In this case, "the poor thing" probably means pity. Then again, it depends on how big these ladies wear their hair and how many teeth are in their head (*and if they're using toothpicks while they talk—a dastardly deed for true Southern women*). These do-no-gooders could definitely be feeling jealous of that fancy truck. (I once read that women wear big hair because they believe it makes them reach closer to heaven. I don't believe it though. I think it's because it makes their *behinds* seem smaller in comparison.)

Suddenly the expression "the poor thing" is popping up everywhere, but it's nothing new. I heard it often when I was a mere child. As in, "Little Lucy is as buck-toothed as Bugs Bunny, the poor thing."

I heard it when I was in a restaurant recently. Two older ladies were talking about a young woman's upcoming wedding. Both of the ladies were what you'd call "hoity toity"—not to be confused with "hoi polloi." They were dressed impeccably, sitting ramrod straight, each with a white linen napkin spread across her lap. Both were drinking white wine and one was dining on Lobster Thermidore (talk about a poor thing—the lobster, that is).

I've read recently where lobsters have feelings too. There's lots of juicy dishing (no pun intended) going on about this subject in the news. It's particularly sad to me because I've always maintained if and when I ever get rich, I'll dine on lobster every day; but darned if the People for Ethical Treatment of Animals (PETA) isn't about to take the joy out of even that. You just can't have any fun anymore!

There's a big debate going on about whether lobsters feel pain when being cooked. A published report last month highlighted scientists from Norway that studied lobsters, crabs, and live worms, all invertebrates (animals without backbones, similar to Howard Stern). They concluded none feels a thing. I already knew that about Howard. But I still wonder how they knew it about lobsters. Maybe they're teaching lobsters sign language just like they do with chimpanzees. "Wave one claw if this hurts and wave two if you're feeling no pain." Come on, how exactly do they know this?

In the same study, Wenche Farstad of the Norwegian School of Veterinary Science in Oslo reiterated that lobsters aren't capable of hurting. Which is to say that Mike Loughlin of the University of Maine was right all along when he pronounced, "It's a semantic thing: no brain, no pain." I am absolutely positive that this study had absolutely nothing to do with the fact that lobstering is the predominant industry in Maine.

Anyway, the PETA folks aren't buying it. They maintain that lobsters do indeed feel pain. They counteracted with, "If we had to drop live pigs or chickens into scalding water, chances are that few of us would eat them." Well, duh! I know I wouldn't. There has got to be a point here, but I honestly don't know what it is.

Well, just so you know, be forewarned. The PETA folks have a whole "Fish Empathy Project" going on. We South Carolinians better hope they don't march down here fishing around for support. If anybody ever attempted to take away my shrimp, scallops, and oysters, *they* would be the ones feeling pain! Don't you think we might be carrying this whole food/nourishment pain thing too far? Next thing you know, we'll have "Save the Collards" protesters showing up at our gardens.

If we continue this charade far enough, we won't have to worry about humans hurting lobsters or collards because we'll be extinct. The collards and lobsters will live on and on, however, free of our threat. The only way they'd die then would be of old age—not being boiled in a pot of water. Give me a break.

I don't think the ladies in the restaurant that day were concerned about lobsters' pain. Instead, they were worried about the aforementioned bride to be. One said the girl was indeed bright... but that was about all she had going for her. She continued, "With a face like that, I never thought she'd find a man, the poor thing!" Her friend nodded in complete agreement, then stabbed a raw oyster in the shell. I wonder if the oyster felt any pain, the poor thing.

Kitchen Table Holds Power for Friends Who Gather 'Round

I have decided that kitchen table friends are the best friends. That old quote really does ring true: "No matter where I serve my guests, it seems they like my kitchen [table] best."

Something magical happens when we sit around the kitchen table with a girlfriend. It softens the rough edges of life and coaxes our timid selves into opening up, freeing us to share our stories and our very lives. It's like a blank slate, complete with chalk—except words are spoken rather than written. I wonder if the enchantment comes from sitting eye-level at the table, which allows us to connect to one another face to face, on the same turf, in a comfy setting. We are no longer bankers, mommies, daughters, secretaries, teachers, lawyers, doctors, or what have you. We lose our labels and are simply friends.

Perhaps it's because the kitchen table is also the place where our bellies *and* souls are fed, for we certainly must have both physical and mental nurturing. Or is it because the table is often the central theme, the heartbeat if you will, of the home? We gather together as one, in communion. I don't think a TV, computer, or cellphone will ever take the place of the kitchen table. At least I hope not.

My best friend, Carolyn, came over today after a luncheon we had attended together. When she walked in, I asked her where she'd like us to sit—at the kitchen table or on my living room sofa. With a huge grin, she said, "Oh, the kitchen table, definitely." It made me pause, thinking how much I liked the idea myself. We then began our tête-à-tête with a mug of steaming hot coffee, topped off with a splash of Kahlua. Not the usual midday beverage for either of us, but maybe our psyches knew we were celebrating many things: friendship, girl power, the gift to gab, and the kinship of sisterhood. It was as if the six-year-old girl inside each of us came alive, eagerly awaiting the ice cream truck.

When I was growing up, my mother had "the girls" over for coffee every morning. Without fail, they would converge at our house, or else at Shirley's, Catherine's, or Anna's. They, too, sat at the kitchen table. No kids were ever allowed in there. If we so much as even poked our heads into the room, we were swooshed away with a firm, "Go outside and play!"

These ladies wanted no distractions when discussing a wide array of subjects. Everything from President Kennedy's assassination to the Cuban Missile Crisis; from how to handle toddler biting, embedded ticks, insolent teenagers, adult acne, and burned casseroles to sharing little tips on how to keep the spark alive in a marriage. Not that they would admit it, but I'm sure gossip was a hot topic, too. For instance, if a new preacher moved into town, my mother and her friends knew the name of the family's china pattern before sundown. If little Joey up the street had a ruptured appendix, his family had a home-cooked meal delivered to their doorstep, even before the doctor finished stitching Joey up.

So today when Carolyn and I sat down, she said to me, "This is what I've always wanted." "What?" I asked. "To sit around the kitchen table and spend time with a good friend," she replied.

We then both reminisced to our childhoods, saying that was exactly what our mothers did. In those days most families had one car and a stay-at-home mom. Perhaps those kitchen table friendships took the place of modern-day therapists, general practitioners, self-improvement lessons, and e-mail chat rooms. Perhaps the expectancy, that sheer delight of having something to look forward to, was a secret to the gathering's success. That, and the familiarity of the intimate group.

The bond that these women formed over the years was strong and impenetrable. The word *trust* was never uttered, but trust was proven time and time again. Their lives weren't perfect, but they were seemingly less complicated, and these women seemed to cope well.

I think we need our girlfriends now more than ever. With the modern-day stress of careers, health issues, school dilemmas, and family dynamics, it seems time spent with a friend at the kitchen table is a good addition to our lives. What really takes place when we meet is a good old-fashioned hen party, complete with laughter, inspiration, security, acceptance, and, if we're lucky, answers to life's problems. This dance of friendship, capped off with a cup of steaming hot coffee, seems a likely duo to snip out those troublesome weeds in life. And everyone has a kitchen table, so there you go! It's free for the asking.

And the kitchen table has served multiple generations well. It's at the kitchen table that weddings have been planned out, finances have been straightened out, divorces have been laid out, goals have been mapped out, clothes patterns have been cut out (and sewn— at least in my home), funerals have been worked out, and surely, lives have been lived out. Oh, the stories these tables could tell!

And think about this: Perhaps the incidences of high blood pressure, migraines, stomach ulcers, spinal strain, and maybe even some cancers would be curbed if we'd start those coffee klatches once more. Just look at how inspired I was after my friend's visit. Now, how do you take your coffee?

CHAPTER 5
Feelings,
Oh, Oh, Oh, Feelings

Don't You Be Messing with My Southern Twang!

I recently read that with the huge influx of Northern folks moving South, our Southern dialect is predicted to die a slow death. First it will be diluted, then drowned, then done *gone*. Hush your mouth! Not that I have anything against "you's guys" for "y'all" or "Bois-tun" instead of Boston. Okay, I lied, I do. Along with pearls, white gloves, parasols, and gardenias, our language is as big a part of our Southern heritage as, say, our vittles: grits, collards, and boiled peanuts. And I aim to preserve it.

Lest this horrible prediction come true, I hereby solemnly swear to do my part to keep Southern colloquialism alive and well. My late, great Granny Pinky (Ida Henrietta Hurtt Morris) was the epitome of Southern grace and charm. Although she didn't speak in tongues, she spoke tongue-in-cheek and had more clichés than Doan's has pills. Granny's brogue was a thick, eastern North Carolina one, at times even sounding like the Harker's Island "hoi toiders."

Granny Pinky entertained certain phrases and ideologies that were unique to her—so much so, that I sometimes had to translate to my friends who sat there dumbstruck. For me, the language she spoke was easy to understand, as common as black flies on a split watermelon at a Fourth of July picnic. But when she'd say, "The good Lord willing and the creek don't rise" I'd tell my puzzled friend Jane DelRosso, who came from Pennsylvania, what she really meant was "if everything goes well."

My sister Cathy and I devised our own Pinkyisms recently, things we remembered that Granny said. They're original and spontaneous.

And though I'm not asking you to "forward" this list via e-mail, I am asking you to make a concerted effort to use at least three of these phrases every single day for the rest of your life. This should ensure our Southern stability, which I'm dubbing Preserving America's Southern Society (PASS), a school of sorts, if you will.

Here we go. Answers are at the end of the column. When you get through reading them, simply read them again and again until they "stick." We'll start off with <u>expressions</u> and then move to words:

1. "Indeed you are not" means:
   a) you'll get a whooping if you do
   b) quit nagging because the answer is "no"
   c) an oxymoron

2. "No one will ever notice" means:
   a) everyone will be staring at you
   b) no one really cares
   c) an oxymoron

3. To "jerk a knot" means:
   a) to tie your john boat up to the dock
   b) a strategy to try to get your chil'ren to behave
   c) to tie on a fashionable scarf

4. "The devil is beating his wife" means:
   a) it's raining while the sun shines
   b) the Dirt Devil is being used to vacuum the hardwood deck outside the single-wide
   c) the wife is losing the race

5. "Putting up damatoes" (tomatoes) means:
   a) placing tomatoes way up high on your refrigerator shelf
   b) canning tomatoes in jars
   c) putting up with tomatoes that are bruised or mealy

6. "Mommock up the furniture" means:
   a) to rearrange a room
   b) to lay askew in a Pawleys Island hammock
   c) tear up the sofa, loveseat, and milk-crate end table

7. The "glove compartment" is:
   a) the tiny box inside the car for storage
   b) the place in the store that sells gloves
   c) another name for "pocket" of the car

8. "The boot" means:
   a) the trunk of your car
   b) footwear for cowboys
   c) pushed aside

Now, let's test your knowledge of certain <u>word pronunciations</u>:

1. How do you say "oil"?
   a) all   b) oy-yul   c) awel

2. How do you say "pen"?
   a) pin   b) pee-yun   c) pan

3. How do you say "roof"?
   a) rhymes with "aloof"   b) rhymes with "hoof"   c) top of the house

4. How do you say "insurance"?
   a) in-shonce   b) in-shor-unz   c) when is the hurricane going to hit?

5. How do you say "umbrella"?
   a) UM-brella   b) um-BRELla   c) parasol

6. How do you say "declare"? as in, "I declare!"
   a) I de-kly-uh   b) I de-clear   c) Idee clare

7. How do you say "river"?
   a) ri-va   b) riv-her   c) ree-ver

8. How do you say "pencil"?
   a) pencil   b) pun-sell   c) pint-sul

Expressions : 1. a   2. b   3. b   4. a   5. b   6. c   7. a and c (fooled ya!)   8. a
Words: 1. b   2. b   3. a   4. b   5. c   6. a   7. a   8. c

So how'd you do? If you scored a perfect 16, you could be an instructor at PASS. If you scored less than 10, you've got a lot of reciting to do. If you scored less than 5, it may be too late. Just kiddin' folks! We love y'all down here, no matter where you're from.

Survey Says: "Sorry, Ma'am, You Don't Qualify"

The strangest thing happened one day this week. I got two telephone survey calls in a row, and I didn't meet either of their qualifications. I know what you're thinking because I thought the same thing. What qualifications? I just figured you had to be a willing fool with a telephone.

Some folks screen all their calls to avoid telephone solicitation, but not me. The minute I realize someone is soliciting, I politely decline and hang up. I refuse to be held "prisoner in communications" by pestering marketers, though I've always been tempted to say, "Tell you what. Why don't you give me *your* phone number and I'll call *you* back at an inconvenient time."

The thing was, I recently got some mail stamped "IMPORTANT!" from the Center for Disease Control and Prevention, hereafter referred to by me as "The Center." It explained that our family had been "specially selected" to take part in a phone survey. Normally dubious, I was surprisingly flattered (yes, I can be a sucker). The more I studied the letter, the more impressed I became. It seemed mysterious and official—government-like, as if I'd been included in an elite group. The letter contained instructions to stay on the phone when the call came for a quick and easy survey.

So when the phone rang two weeks later, I decided why not, thinking I could be a good sport. What harm could it be? I told the woman (perhaps too eagerly) that I had been expecting her call, and I did indeed have some free time in which to be interviewed. However, the *few* minutes the letter promised dragged into fifteen minutes as I answered boring and generic questions—nothing at all delicate or highly confidential, as I'd expected.

She began by asking me how many people lived in our home, our age, gender, and race. In the final category, I had six choices, which she read out loud. I stopped her after the first choice, which was the right one, but she said standard policy was to *state each choice*. She continued reading number two through six. Now I was positive this was the work of the government! I rolled my eyes as she went through this scenario three times: for me, for my husband, Russell, and our college-aged daughter, Katie. This was getting monotonous after all. I couldn't help but wonder what was next.

After getting our family "stats" right, she asked me how many telephones we had. "What the —?" I began to say. It seemed so irrelevant. Frankly, I couldn't see the correlation between telephones and gram positive bacteria, unless you could catch a disease from the bacteria on your phone. *Was that it?!* I wondered. I began tallying up our cellphones and landlines out loud. "Well, let's see. We have three cellphones. We have —" but she didn't let me finish. She said emphatically. "How many telephone numbers does your home have, connected to a jack in your wall?" I wanted to say, "Standard policy is I *count them all!*" but I didn't have the nerve. She should explain in detail what she wanted before she asked, don't you think? Finally I replied, "one," sounding pitiful. "One?" she repeated. "Sorry, you don't qualify. Thank you!" Click. And that was it. She hung up without so much as a goodbye, better luck next time, or your consolation prize is in the mail. This makes me wonder, what does it take to qualify? And though this one isolated incident may seem annoying by normal standards, just wait, there's more!

Before my rejection had settled in, the phone rang again. I am not making this up. This time it was a woman with the Gallup Poll who wanted me to answer a few simple questions. Funny thing, I'd always wanted to be included in a Gallup Poll, or maybe even the Nielsen ratings! Was this my lucky day? My excitement must have shown. What am I saying? I was downright easy—a survey pushover. "Shoot!" I said to her, almost giddy. "Excuse me?" she asked. I replied, "I mean, fire away, I'm all yours," smiling from ear to ear.

That was when I thought I heard a snort—a nasally laughing sound. Unlike the lady with "The Center," the only personal question she asked me was, "Are you over age 18?" I almost said, "Yeah, three times that much," but that wasn't true and no woman in her right mind exaggerates her age. Next, she inquired about how often

I shopped at a certain mega-giant, super-savings store. (Hint: They did not build in Murrells Inlet, and Chevy Chase's car ended up in their parking lot in the movie "Christmas Vacation.") Her second question was when was the last time I had visited *that* store. This was really freaky because I had just left there two hours ago. I wondered if she secretly knew this...but how? She continued, "Which location, John's Island?" (which made absolutely no sense because that's over two hours away from my home).

I wanted to scream "In the Twilight Zone, which I'm in right now!" She cleared this up, saying, "Which location, which town?" dragging out the word *towwwwwwwnnn* and sounding awfully irritated. I replied, "Surfside Beach." After several seconds, she located the store on her list. I thought, *Finally, we're getting somewhere.* But she must have been in cahoots with "The Center" caller. At that moment she apologized, saying, "Sorry, you don't qualify. That store's recently been polled." I hung up with an audible gasp, shook my head, and blinked back a tear.

It's a sad occasion for a willing fool with a telephone to be rejected by a telemarketer, but to have it happen twice in one day? I can only hope the Nielsen folks will be easier on me.

Clear and Present Dangers
Almost Halt Yard Work

Ever since I read that pine nuts (and not money, darn it!) grow on trees, I've been outside, inspecting my pine trees. At $20 per pound, I'd be a millionaire if I harvested a crop. Not really, but I have been in the yard picking up those prickly, ugly, menacing monstrous byproduct of pine trees: pine cones. I can't figure out what purpose pine cones serve other than to provide seeds for new pine trees (what a shame those cute little pine tassels can't do the job), to thus produce even more irritating pine cones. It's a vicious cycle.

I can't stand pine cones! Even when wearing gloves, sharp edges cut and maim well-meaning, innocent gardeners like myself. I've made it my mission in life (or at least in my yard) to get rid of them. I'm aware that the simplest solution would be to cut down all of our pine trees, but since we have nearly thirty of them, we've never called the tree man. I figure for what it would cost us to get rid of them, we could buy a new lot, clear all the trees, and build a new home.

Now, oak trees—oh honey, that is an entirely different matter. I love oak trees! They are regal, massive, and sturdy, withstanding the test of time to live to be several hundred years old. I've often said I'd buy a lot or existing home just to enjoy the perfect oak tree. Plus, along with magnolias, gardenias, and camellias, oak trees represent the Old South so well. There's nothing prettier than a tree-lined dirt lane with massive oaks on either side.

After our extremely windy March, Russell and I have been trying for days to restore our yard to something that resembles a lawn rather than a forest, which it had turned into. We've picked up limbs, leaves, assorted trash, and yes, pine cones, until our backs are breaking and our hands are raw. I almost didn't insist upon the spring yard cleaning this year because I've been reading and hearing about wild critters nearby that—well, quite frankly, frighten me.

I read in the newspaper recently where a lady in a nearby county was "attacked" by a bobcat. Aside from the obvious danger, it made me wonder what, exactly, is a bobcat? Is it like a raccoon, possum, squirrel, or a regular old house cat? I've lived in the South all my life, so sure, I've heard of them, but I've never seen one. And what is this creature's real name—bobcat sounds like a nickname!

In the "woman versus bobcat" article, I read where this woman courageously (but unwisely, in my opinion) fought off this bad boy for a solid fifteen minutes with a rake. Luckily, her neighbor came to her rescue. The 60-something-year-old woman in peril certainly put up a courageous fight—but for what? Well, it turns out the woman was protecting puppies that the bobcat was annoying. She spotted the animal from her window and went outside under her own free will to protect the pups. But people, listen up! She wouldn't be around long enough to watch these puppies grow (much less protect them) if the bobcat had had his way. *No siree.* If I ever see a wild animal outside my window, I'm calling a game warden or an animal control officer. Somebody! Anybody with power. I'm sure not going to take matters into my own hands, rake or no rake.

Then another nature scare: My next door neighbor, April, my sweet friend with the gorgeous, thick hair and the lovely singing voice, called me. Nearly in hysterics, she asked if I had seen any snakes in my yard. Eeeeeew! I told her about three years ago I saw a small snake near our heat pump, but he slithered away. In a high-pitched, nervous tone, April told me she had seen not one, but *two* snakes in her yard within three days. She killed them both because she was pretty sure they were poisonous. Then she asked me if I knew what a poisonous snake looked like. I said I sure did: "Scary!"

With prickly pine cones, beastly bobcats, and scary snakes, maybe I should stay in the house permanently. That's a shame, since spring just sprung! Well, I could always put up a sign like I did when I was five years old. I walked into the house one day and asked my mama how to spell "allowed." She asked me why I wanted to know and I said, "Because I'm making a sign to put on the clothes line that says, 'No bees allowed!'" I wished I hadn't just thought of that; I'd forgotten that the season for honeybees, wasps, and hornets is just around the corner. If it's not one thing, it's two, or three, or four!

Saving and Savoring "Family" Christmas Cards

Two weeks after Christmas, Russell asked me what I planned to do with "that pile of Christmas cards" that had been stashed in a wicker basket on the fireplace hearth.

Maybe I'm overly sentimental, but I like holding onto holiday cards (and other cards, too). In our family, it's a tradition for Kelly to read through the cards when she visits. She gets a kick out of checking up on old friends. Each Christmas, she'll sit down with me on our Christmassy-red sofa; take her time poring over each card, and make enthusiastic comments as I sit nearby. "So, the Blantons are now living in Beaufort?" Or else, "Omigosh, when did Emmie Lou stop making fishing nets?" But she gets the most excited when photos are included—and truth be told, so do I! In that case, she'll say, "My, when did Kennedy get so tall?" Or "Boy, do I feel old. I taught Chandler at Myrtle Beach Primary twelve years ago. Now he's in college." We both become disappointed and puzzled when the parents are not in the photo, but only the children.

If it's a family Christmas card, we want to see the *entire family* and it really is a letdown without everyone. I compare it to cooking dinner for the kids and not joining in the meal yourself, or planning your child's birthday party and then leaving your house, just as the guests arrive. Everybody can join in the fun of Christmas snapshots! So what if we parents have lost some youth and vitality, compared to our children? What's the big deal about gaining a few pounds or *sprouting* a few gray hairs—or *losing* a few hairs, for that matter? I say, "Who cares?" Don't keep your friends and family in suspense—show us what you look like now! Most of us parents have been through several changes since high school and childbirth. That's what makes the photos so charming (and irresistible).

This year Kelly sent a Christmas postcard family photo—a great idea—which I have displayed on my refrigerator. And she began a new tradition. When she came to visit me, she brought the current Christmas cards she'd received. That was exciting, seeing photos of her friends from college or from her current neighborhood, and reading their latest news.

Speaking of photos, my neighbor Kim Teeples asked me in December to take an outdoors one of her family—her two darling boys, her husband, and herself—for a Christmas card. Charlie and Will were dressed alike in shirts and rolled-up blue jeans and barefooted. Darling! Kim had on a stylish poncho and Lamont was his usual handsome self. It was reassuring to know someone else likes to have the entire family in the picture. I snapped three to four times, the usual straight-on shot. Then I knelt down and pushed the zoom lens, saying, "Now I'll get really creative. I've been known to lie down on the ground or step up on a bench to get just the right angle."

They smiled and laughed. I said, "Hold it right there! Perfect!" But the main button wouldn't push down after repeated attempts; it seemed stuck. Kim didn't move. She stared straight ahead, smiling through clenched teeth, which gave her a ventriloquist/dummy look. "I wonder what's wrong? Boys, sit still!" The camera jammed. Kim was distraught, saying that she has the worst luck with cameras. "So do I," I mumbled. But she went ahead and rattled off the list of negatives—no pun intended—saying she is either out of film, the batteries are dead, or she forgets to bring the camera along. That is *exactly* what happens to me (once, I even dropped a camera on concrete). Kim said she had just taken photos that very morning and couldn't understand why it wouldn't work since fourteen exposures were remaining. I offered later that day to retake them, but after buying new film, the babysitter took them.

But getting back to Russell's earlier question: I said to him, "I'm going to save the cards. I plan to put them in my nightstand drawer with the others." He looked dubious. "Why?" I told him, "Because one day when I'm old and gray and all alone, I'll enjoy looking back through them." He asked, "Alone?! Where am I going to be?" For once in my life I was speechless. He had a good point.

Finally I came to my senses and hugged him, saying, "Oh honey! You know what I mean. You'll either be playing golf or taking a nap inside while I sit in a rocker on the old folk's home porch. I didn't mean *alone* alone. Really." He shrugged and walked away slowly.

I don't know what it is about cards that make me so emotional, which isn't in my general make-up, but I like to keep them close by. Even my daughters don't save their cards permanently. Oh sure, they check them carefully for gifts of money before they toss them out, but they are good-as-gone once the note is read.

For me, cards reinforce my optimistic belief of having good friends and family to support you through the bad times and to cheer you during the good times. It's a written reminder—a souvenir, if you will. And no, it doesn't have to be a Hallmark card. Some of my favorites are those "two for a dollar." I'm not embarrassed to tell you that's about all I send out these days.

I just bought six Valentine cards (don't tell Russell, but one is for him!). I wonder if he'll save that one since I pointed out the benefit of saving cards and looking through them when he's old and gray…and all alone. Nah, 'cause he'll have me there to hound him *in person*, so I guess he'd argue "What's the point?"

Leaving Plane Phobia Behind

When my friend Kimi called, inviting me to speak and sign books at her sorority meeting in Springdale, Arkansas, I jumped at the chance—then I panicked! I asked myself, "What have I done?" After all, that meant *flying*, and I hadn't flown in thirteen years, not since a business trip on a small, company plane. I nearly passed out from claustrophobia then. In fact, I never flew until age twenty-six. Take-off horrified me with the plane's sharp, vertical incline and the shrill, cicada-like engine noise. I was plane "phobic."

We met Kimi and Timi, forty-something-year-old twins, when Russell and I went on a Carnival Cruise. As always, we *drove* to Port Canaveral. I reasoned that driving was more economical: a motel bill and a couple of meals versus two plane tickets. In truth, I avoided air travel at all costs, worrying about things like a wheel falling off, the pilot falling asleep, or the cabin pressure falling.

On the cruise, before we'd ever laid eyes on the twins, folks asked, "Have you seen the twins—the beautiful, tan, shapely twins who wear hot pink or turquoise?" One said, "Picture blonde Delta Burkes." Another said, "I believe they're stars, traveling incognito."

I searched everywhere for signs of the divine diva duo. On the second night, just before we entered a cocktail party, the elevator opened and out they stepped. I felt faint, like a giddy high-school kid with a crush. These dazzling twins were surrounded by their "staff," I surmised—a manager, agent, press secretary, and fashion consultant (they later turned out to be friends and family). Their million-dollar smiles, genteel Southern drawls, and raspy, boisterous laughter intrigued me. Over the next five days, we bonded like sisters. I learned they weren't movie stars after all, but rather, smart, passionate women with families, active in their community, with careers "on hold."

We chatted over Bahama Mamas on the pool deck at sunset, remarking how similar our childhoods were, growing up in family-owned businesses. We posed for photos at a luau, sharing stories of birthing babies, best friends, and birthday bashes. We attended parties, discussing the merit of hair extensions and the bother of organic gardening. On the final day, no one wanted to leave. We cried and hugged and cried some more, promising to keep in touch through e-mails and phone calls, pledging to one day meet again.

Flash forward one year to Kimi's phone call. Even though my lips said "Yes," my heart skipped a beat, sensing possible flying fiascos: standing in long lines for hours at security, setting off an alarm with my chunky silver jewelry, and alerting drug dogs who sniffed out my birth control pills.

Several months passed before Timi verified the date. In the meantime, I worried. On the one hand, I certainly wanted to see the twins. On the other, I did not want to fly! Asking Timi to book my flight made me feel better. Hey, if I didn't even want to think about flying, how could I talk intelligently about flying? Now, understand, I had no fear of traveling alone, speaking in front of seventy-some women, or being gone from home a full week—I just didn't want to zoom 30,000 feet in the air to do it.

A good friend said, "You'll be fine, just take a Xanax before boarding. Everyone does."

"Even the pilot?" I asked, my voice cracking.

To add to my pre-flight anxiety, my itinerary was rather complicated. Flying out of Myrtle Beach meant three layovers and nine hours of travel. Instead, I picked an easier flight out of Wilmington, and I visited my parents in Jacksonville, North Carolina, the day before. When we went to the airport, darned if we didn't get lost. Running late and nearly starving, we skidded into the parking lot, only to discover the airport restaurant was closed for remodeling! I prayed that the runway, air traffic tower, or cockpit weren't also being remodeled. Then Mom asked, "Where are you sitting on the plane?"

I glanced at my ticket. "Oh, in the middle, it looks like."

"Good!" she said. "That's supposed to be the safest place." *Right*, I thought. After all, Mom flew to Hawaii in 1964 and then to Las Vegas ten years ago. I get my "infrequent flyer" status honest.

I said goodbye, then Dad pried my hands loose from his shoulders. I nervously inched my way through the jet way, being denied any possible (and perhaps final?) breath of fresh air. Finally, I boarded that big, bad jet.

Five pretzels and a few ounces of cola later, I thought, *Piece of cake* (even though of course they never served any). But when we later landed thirty minutes late, I couldn't find my friends.

"Yoo hoo! Sweetie! Over here!" Kimi soon squealed. My eyes watered with the exhilaration of seeing her again—that, and I needed a bathroom.

After dinner, they drove me to the Hampton Inn where they spoiled me rotten with a humongous gift basket and floral arrangements in hot pink and turquoise. They also inspected my room, making sure it was perfect—non-smoking, two queen size beds (heck, I *felt* like a queen!), then offered to help me unpack. I slept like a baby and woke up feeling refreshed.

The next day, after lunch, their friend dropped me off at the motel. But when I walked into the lobby, I shook my head, thinking, *Where am I?* Something was different. The front desk was on the wrong side, the breakfast area was gone, and there were new plants hanging on every balcony. I felt disoriented, and to make matters worse, my feet hurt. I tried to call Kimi on my cellphone, but had no reception. So, I walked outside and that's when I saw the sign that said Holiday Inn Express. Sitting perpendicular, fifty yards away, was my motel, The Hampton Inn. *What's next?* I thought. What if I ended up getting dropped off at the bus station instead of the airport terminal? What if this whole trip was a dream, and I didn't really get on that plane in Wilmington after all?

Before leaving the Springdale airport, I discovered a problem. My flight was overbooked, meaning I'd be arriving five hours late, at 10 p.m. Thinking this could work to my advantage, I asked about a direct flight to Jacksonville and surprisingly, that worked.

On the flight home, I met another new friend, an orthodontist who was looking for a speaker for her dental group, also in Arkansas. I gladly accepted the invitation, even though I'll be flying again. That's okay. After all, it seems there's more to worry about these days on the ground than in the *air*, especially for me.

The Wide Range of Change

One of my favorite quotes (author unknown) is, "The only thing constant in life is change." Don't we know it?! Baby-boomers, babies, Generation X, and aging parents—no one can escape the inevitability of change. Those of us who were born in the 1950s have seen, heard, or done it all, and sometimes all three. From Ouija Boards to Weejuns to Woodstock!

What's a person to do with all this change? Well, what else can you do but *go with the flow? Accept the inevitable. Don't worry, be happy; things could always be worse. Don't sweat the small stuff. Adapt. Breathe!*

The world of fashion is not exempt from all this change. In fact, some people might argue that our clothing designers are at the helm of this frenzied phenomenon of constant change. A recent article published in *The Sun News* written by Jackie White entitled "Girlie Look Now at Front," but subtitled "Trend may have limited long-term boomer appeal" (hmmmm…) caught my attention. It says that the world of chic is "anchored in the middle of the most feminine era we've seen in a long while." *What does this mean?* (That's currently a favorite cliché in my house, although I'm sure even that will wear out and change to some other cliché in due time.)

Does this high-falluting femininity mean those bulky denim and for sure, non-flattering overalls are now out, as in, out of style? Somebody better tell that restaurant (nameless) down in Murrells Inlet, whose waitresses wear dungaree overalls as a uniform. On second thought, I'm afraid it wouldn't be too feminine to be serving chicken wings in barbecue sauce, while draping a ruffly sleeve through that sticky mess, or dripping ice-cold beer from frosted mugs down their now-exposed cleavage.

My favorite line in this article was "Are the fashion folks simply trying to entice women who already have closets full of tailored lean black pants, T-shirts, and tank tops?" I'll answer that. Uh huh. That would be me. And my reply to that question, by the way, is an unequivocal yes! The new look is being called "Bohemian fashion." And please let's not get that wrong, lest we be totally uncool. Now, I just have to share this with y'all: Several weeks before I read this article (clairvoyant hippie-chick that I am) I purchased a gorgeous Renee Derby two-piece blouse and tank top, all-flowery and ruffly, with a sexy, plunging neckline. This was specifically matched-up to my soft, brushed cotton (hopefully still-fashionable) cranberry capris.

As it turned out, I ended up paying an alterations lady to re-make the blessed thing because the tank top hung all wrong at the neck line. I'd fluff up the paper-thin material and it would sag back down. I'd twist and turn the itsy-bitsy ruffle edged collar and it would turn inward. The lining kept showing. And it also had a dar-ling beaded-like little string-thing that had come unsewn, which also had to be repaired with a hook-and-eye. I'm so glad I was able to pay twice over to know I am now a bonafide "girlie girl"! (Nobody said keeping up with change would be cheap.)

In "Changes in Latitudes, Changes in Attitudes," Jimmy Buffett sings, "These changes in latitudes, changes in attitudes; Nothing remains quite the same. Through all of the islands and all of the highlands, If we couldn't laugh we would all go insane." You sing it, Jimmy! They say there is a fine line between laughter and tears. We're stressed-out, all right, with all these changes, but laughter can't hurt. People all over the country are forming laughing clubs. Internet Web sites have daily jokes that people are more addicted to than horoscopes. Comedy Central is the prevailing TV channel in my house when Katie, our twenty-one year old, is home. As for me, I feel privileged to travel and speak as both a humorist and author.

Still, I've not always accepted change in the graceful way I am suggesting everyone else should. For instance, when SUVs first came out, I sounded like Mama in "Mama's Family," the old CBS show, saying, "I wouldn't own one of those things. No sir! They're too nar-row, they ride funny, and I hear they flip over just like that," snapping my fingers at the word "that."

Now look at me. Ten years later I've joined the other crazy fools, but I'm sitting up high and mighty in my Kia Sportage, feeling like a trucker. That's got to be the enticement, sitting up high. It's pure power! That is my favorite part, being able to see past the car ahead of me. Providing it's not a bigger SUV than mine, like that fancy, brand-new Yukon my brother, Steve, drives! (It's like a jet-plane inside with all those fancy buttons and measurements, gauges and readouts. Cool!) Or providing it's not a van or a mini-bus. Hey, does anybody out there own a car anymore?

This change thing is creeping into our homes as well. Anybody buy a new DVD, CD burner, or MIDI player in the last day or two? Sorry, it's already outdated. Something new is already on the shelves, or will be tomorrow. *The Old Farmer's Almanac 2002* tells us to be aware of sweeping changes (no pun intended) with the broom—like I care! They say that along with brushes, dust cloths, buckets, and mops, brooms are showing up in iMac colors like blueberry, grape, tangerine, kiwi green, and cherry red.

And get this: They say that kids who used to play school can now pretend to be CEOs, thanks to a California manufacturer who has a line of ergonomically correct and brightly colored chairs and desks for kids who have nowhere to go but up! Really. Lastly, we are told of alarm clocks that do anything but buzz. You can now wake up to prayers, stand-up comedy routines, Zen gongs, crashing ocean waves, and (oh no!) barking dogs.

Okay, here's some advice from me: Don't sit still too long, lest you be left behind. You've got books/articles/internet updates to read, ruffles and other feminine things to shop for, and SUVs to test-drive.

Independence Is a State of Mind, Not a Promotion

The mysterious message read, "You are next in line for promotion in your firm." Having read my Chinese fortune cookie, I tucked it in my purse, planning to add it to my collection. That's why I dine so often in Chinese restaurants: to gain insight into my future, plot my goals and aspirations, see what marvelous events are just around the corner—and because I love General Tso's chicken.

Truth is, I consider myself a forward-thinking person, open to ideas and change if I can better myself. Yet I'm fiercely independent and enjoy doing things my own way. (Did I mention stubborn?) Still, I found this whole concept intriguing. It got me thinking about re-assessing my life, in a manner of speaking.

As it stands now, I own my own home, my own car, and my own business. Twenty-six years ago I was lucky enough to find the near-perfect mate, and with him I feel complete: an equal half of a whole, free but united, independent but in partnership. I've been told I'm a responsible, intelligent, accountable adult. I'd say my life is pretty comfy and I feel very blessed. So why is it that I sometimes fall for those silly prophetic traps? You might think a realistic, confident woman would shun such nonsense. You might be wrong. Anyway, it's all in fun! I also read my horoscope, have checked out Tarot cards, and once even had my palm read. On the other hand, I realize none of these predictions is scientifically proven.

But back to this fortune cookie "promotion in my firm." I am just wondering when this advancement is going to happen. Every morning I wake up, shower, and walk down the hall to my home-office a few minutes early to win over the boss (me). Fast and furious, I type at the speed of light to impress the boss (me). If I really want to be extra-good, I skip lunch and keep on working to earn brownie points with the productivity-obsessed boss (me). At the end of the work day I clock-out, so to speak, and tell the boss (me) goodbye in my cheeriest voice, along with "Have a nice evening!"

Well, maybe this time the cookie is wrong. It's starting to look as if there's no promotion in sight. Hard as I try to impress me, it's just not working. I'm listed on my tax forms as "owner," but maybe I could promote myself to CEO or CFO (Chief Female Officer). But even if I do get promoted, what's the benefit? Will I get a raise? Will I be better off? Oh, this plague of self-doubt!

I mean it's not as if I'm unhappy in my present position. After all, there are many advantages to being self-employed: time flexibility, being your own boss, control of policies and procedures, wearing casual clothes. But self-promotion? I'd never thought about it until that fateful day when I read that cookie and realized my whole career could change in the blink of an eye!

I was even thinking recently, with July 4 nearly upon us, how grateful I am to live in the good ole United States of America, a country chock-full of freedom and opportunities, where anything is possible—to conceive, believe, achieve—if we set our minds to it. *"Land of the free and home of the brave."* So what if I get caught up every now and then with a mysterious message in the form of a Chinese fortune cookie? It helps me to dream! Without dreams, there is no action. I heard a popular author say she constantly asks, "What if?" to give her stories life. We should do the same thing for ourselves.

When I arrived home from the restaurant, I took the fortune cookie message out of my purse and read it again. Then I filed it with the others; in fact, right next to "Don't race to your destination—appreciate the scenery." Kind of ironic, I thought.

That's when it all made sense. My life is fine just the way it is. Independence, as I understand it, means *simply being me*—a nonconformist, which in turn allows me the freedom to live my life as an individual. And yes, I appreciate the scenery every single day. It's true, I may not attend big board meetings, drive around in a shiny, new company car, or have a lavish expense account. But this life, just as it is, is good enough for me. I'm happy. No promotion in the world could change that!

Past, Present, Future:
Photos Give Us Cause to Pause

Old photos fascinate me. I can sift through them for hours, reminiscing about one occasion or another. If the occasion took place before my birth, I conjure up a setting. For instance, the time period (perhaps the Great Depression); the location (vacationing at the beach); or the events of a particular day (the sinking of the *Titanic*). I often feel a flood of emotion, in awe of the power of a photograph. I've discovered that, like an old song or a fine wine, photos are indeed mood altering.

I look with tenderness at a picture of my then-elderly great-grandmother Etta. She is wearing a neck brace, the result of an unfortunate fall. Her hair is beautiful—silver, wavy, and slightly disheveled. A photo of my mother makes me swell with pride. In this one, she's a young mother, but is amazingly fit in her plaid, two-piece bathing suit (a stylish halter top, even!)—no doubt, something she herself sewed.

In my home, entire walls adorn photos of my family spanning many years. Though I have several in assorted frames displayed on the piano and various tables, the wall photos tell a story. In the hallway, I have eleven large framed photos of "us": Russell, Kelly, Katie, and myself. If I ever need a good laugh, I stare in disbelief at the one of me from early in our marriage. I am wearing a curly perm. *Lord, what was I thinking?* I should've known better.

My hair is naturally as straight as a stick—a fact I was reminded of each time my mother gave me a Lilt home perm. I nearly passed out from the rotten eggs-like vapor, and for what? All that suffering and not one ever "took." After the first washing, I bawled like a baby. In those days, my dream was to become a movie star and no decent movie star had *straight* hair.

If I want to feel nostalgic, I pick out the church portrait where Katie, at age eight (now a college senior), had ringlets. Yes, I styled her straight hair with the curling iron. I am my mother after all. In this photo, I quickly notice her monstrous grosgrain hair bow, two oversized "Bugs Bunny" teeth, and a striped chintz dress. Next, a feeling of peace washes over me when I spot the photo of Kelly and Chuck on their honeymoon, a short eight years ago. Kelly's dream was to have a happy home complete with a husband and two children—and though she doesn't have the white picket fence, her home is much grander than mine.

Finally, there is Russell. This one elicits feelings of warmth and wonder. Steady as a rock, salt of the earth, handsome and shy. Sequential photos show the gradual graying (and charm) of his hair over the years. I'm sure I was the cause of more than a few of those grays. The most recent additions, our granddaughters Madison, age four, and Carly, age four months, show sisters lying on a baby blanket, face to face, communicating like only sisters can, sprawled, entangled arms and legs with happy smiles.

Farther back in our home in the master bedroom, a certain wall begged, *Pick me!* some years ago, and so I did. There, I have photos of my life from infancy through young adulthood with my family of origin: Mom, Dad, Cathy, Nancy, me, and Steve. These are all black and white and they have a story of their own. They reveal serious posed portraits as well as more relaxed, candid home shots. They also show a family who was proud as proud could be. I can almost see my father's chest sticking out in one example, his hands folded just so. He is young, thin, angular-jawed and with deep-set, serious eyes. Mom's hair is coiffed perfectly, earbobs in place. She is wearing a stylish dress. And though each of us show slight smiles, Steve—the baby and an Opie Taylor look-alike—is just a second away from a full blown hee-haw of laughter.

A favorite photo is of us siblings, sitting on the steps of the old Bootery store in downtown New Bern, North Carolina, where Dad worked as a young man. I'm holding a new doll. Steve is dressed as a cowboy, complete with boots and a holster, one pants leg hiked up. Cathy, a demure teenager, wears a fashionable cashmere sweater. Nancy is holding a doll, a smaller, dressier version of mine.

An outdoor photo taken at Easter time shows our 1957 Chevy

as the backdrop where we sisters posed in bonnets, patent leather shoes, and identical poodle skirts that Mom made.

Once when visiting my parents' North Carolina home, I went through several photo albums, picking out stacks of pictures I wanted copied. Dad graciously offered to do this since he knew of a photo lab. A week later he gave me the bad news. The lab could copy them, but without the negatives, the cost was exorbitant: $400! I don't know what was most disappointing, hearing the cost, not getting the photos after all, or (and this was probably it) having to painstakingly file them all back, one by one.

Photos represent something else: a timeline of our past, present, and perhaps, future. I know I inherited my father's skinny legs and my mother's clear-blue yes. But I wonder if I'll grow into Granny Pinky's regal and impressive stature. Will I one day gather an entire family of fourteen (like my parents did in 1989) for a portrait?

Photos. Family. Love. They kind of all go together. And though life is never perfect, I enjoy taking stock of those old photographs now and then. It keeps things in perspective. And heck, if I'm ever feeling blue, one glimpse of that bad perm and I realize things could always be worse!

New Year's Resolutions?
Not When Chocolate Rules!

I purposely waited a full week *after* New Year's Day to announce my New Year's resolutions. For good reason, too. I thought I could outsmart myself. Let me explain: I figured by mastering the highest-priority resolution (lose weight and shape up through proper nutrition and exercise) for a good while—I'm talking since *September*—this would ensure success. Then when I said it out loud in January, it would have already been happening. Sneaky? Perhaps. Reverse psychology? Maybe. But not altogether without merit. It's complicated, but I'm competitive by nature and more so with myself than anyone else. I don't like to fail at things, and I don't accept defeat particularly well. Plus, there is something rather virtuous about accomplishing goals that we set for ourselves. Maybe it's because we can give ourselves a pat on the back, a self-thumbs up, or a self-wink. Actually, hollering "You go, girl!" knowing that you just *did* is an awesome feeling.

The thing is, I had started working out regularly again at Health Point this past September with all good intentions. I'd slacked off during the summer, opting to walk occasionally on the beach instead—not at a particularly brisk pace, I might add. In other words, I got lazy. So, I made an appointment with my assigned exercise physiologist, Angela. She did a full reassessment on me, much to my chagrin. Here's why: If you want to talk about being humbled, just let a smart, attractive, in-shape twenty-something-year-old tanned blonde measure your hips and thighs. I'm glad the folks working at the gym have great ethics and high moral standards. Otherwise, they could make a lot of money selling the client's personal numbers! Well, at least mine would be easy to remember: forty-forty-forty. But then again, who would care?

I was doing pretty good on my "New Me" workout until Thanksgiving. As usual, we went out of town to visit family. And being out of town means no workouts. I justify this by saying I am there to visit family (and shop and eat out, all the important stuff!) and there's no time for anything else (plus, three passes around Triangle Towne Center burns up lots of calories). For our Thanksgiving meal (which served sixteen guests) I counted the dishes at Kelly's house in Raleigh. They numbered twenty-six! There was so much food, in fact, that it was placed in several locations: dining room table, kitchen table, countertops, on top of the refrigerator, and the fireplace mantle. Still, I came home more determined than ever and kept up with my daily trek of going to the gym.

Then the Christmas holidays came and I found myself severely lacking in self-restraint, will power, and creativity. I *tried* to pick healthy choices. For instance, I ate lots of celery. It is, after all, cruciferous and a great "detergent" food. (I learned *that* in dental hygiene school many years ago.) Sad to say, my celery was stuffed with rich cream cheese, mayonnaise, and olives (a family recipe). I ate lean, low-fat, fresh turkey…slathered with hefty, full-bodied, greasy gravy. I rounded out my platter with what was to be colorful, healthy green beans. I'm not sure, but I think I caught a glimpse of someone (who?) spooning a couple of dollops of bacon grease in the pot. Every dish that seemed benign turned out to be bogus. Sweet potatoes? Full of beta-carotene, right? Yes. But they were also full of butter, maple syrup, marshmallows, and pecans. What about that healthy broccoli packed with Vitamin A and C? Well, those vitamins were probably duking it out with melted butter and drizzled cheese.

I'm finding that the New Year's resolution I have set may indeed take the entire year to achieve, simply to correct the recent two weeks of insulin shock my body is suffering. Depending on how I look at it, this was the best year or worst year for Christmas and New Year goodies. Everywhere I turned I was offered peanut butter balls, chocolate fudge, macadamia nut mix, lemon bars, and various pies and cakes. One particular cup of coffee I was served had real whipping cream floating atop the steaming hazelnut treat. (Oh, and did I mention our nephew Jason Ipock's wedding to Sarah Metz on New Year's Eve? They had an impressive reception loaded with rich food selections.)

Here's an idea for an alternative in the future: The week before Christmas all the way up to the week after New Year's, just slide me up to an IV pole with dripping glucose about three times a day. Maybe that way I won't be tempted to eat ten pounds of sugar and fat daily. And I know I'm not alone in this thinking. My regular friends at Health Point (namely Doris, Janice, Kate, Roz, Margaret, Grace, Eric, and Richard), a few others, and myself pretty much sweated bullets on the Precor, the treadmill, and the Stairmaster—then confessed later to consuming gobs of goodies at recent parties, open houses, family meals, and the like.

Oh no! I've just realized the pigging out is not over. We're headed out tomorrow to our annual Morris family reunion at Emerald Isle, North Carolina, for four days. And folks are begging me to bring my yummy Congo Squares. So, perhaps this second week of January also isn't the perfect time to time to announce (or stick to) New Year's resolutions. Maybe I should wait until January is over and try for February. But then again, Valentine's Day comes and chocolate rules once again!

CHAPTER 6
Let's Get Physical, or Perhaps Metaphysical

When You Travel and Your Luggage Doesn't, SHOP!

My parents came to our home recently for a three-day visit from North Carolina. After a filling dinner and a double-rich chocolate dessert that left us moaning, we moved into the living room to relax and watch some TV. After a while it was time to slip on my pajamas, but when I came out of my bedroom I saw something strange. Mom and Dad were huddled in the hallway whispering, hands flailing, faces contorted. I knew something really weird was going on. "What's up?" I said, more than a little curious.

"Your father forgot my *carry-on bag*," Mom said, rolling her eyes, head tilted in his direction.

"Carry-on bag?" I asked. Trying to add a little humor, I told her that sounded like she'd arrived by airplane, not car. Big mistake. Mom glared at me as Dad chirped in with his version. "Your mother forgot her *suitcase*." Now *he* was the one rolling his eyes. Uh oh. I wasn't "going there," so I tiptoed on past them while they continued dissecting the problem. I overheard parts of sentences—quick, huffy phrases, like, "didn't leave it in the usual spot," "you're always in a hurry," and "didn't check behind me."

Forgotten luggage—every traveler's worst nightmare. I imagine the only thing worse than forgetting your luggage—say, while on a swanky vacation to Belize—would be forgetting to bring your spouse along. Or do you think that might be too obvious?

Actually I'm one of those people who wish my luggage would get lost by the airlines. Never mind the fact that I rarely fly—*if I were flying*, that's what I'd wish. That's because I figure I could get some new outfits at the airline's expense, and what woman in her right mind wouldn't love to toss out the old and reel in the new? As they say, "Everything is negotiable!"

That's more or less what I said to Mom when I got up the nerve to butt in. "Just think, Mom, now Dad can buy you three new outfits, one for each day of your visit." Her curt reply to me was, "I don't want new clothes. I want my old clothes!" Go figure. Plus, she was having too much fun watching Dad squirm. Funny thing was he wasn't really squirming at all. By then he had gone into the living room and was sacked out in the easy chair.

Thinking back, I had noticed when they arrived that afternoon that Dad only made two quick trips from our house to their car, to bring in everything. When I asked him could I help, he said, "Nah. Thanks. We didn't bring all that much." If he'd only known...

That night Mom discovered, little by little, what she didn't have. What she did have included her cosmetics case and a hang-up bag with a nice suit for Sunday. Other than that, she had only the clothes on her back: a white shirt, blue jeans, and Keds. But she didn't have her favorite silky blue pajamas, and when it came time for bed, she and I scrounged around for something comfy. When I got through "clothing" her, it was, well, a sight. She wore Russell's brand-new XXL tee shirt from a cruise that read, "Southern Living at Sea," it depicted green and pink fish and aqua-colored islands. (Well, we do live near the beach!) Never mind that it hung down to her knees, almost totally covering my red Victoria's Secret P.J. bottoms that she wore. (She didn't want to wear the top that matched them, saying, "I'd burn up in that material!") She also had on my black furry slippers with the rhinestones. It was a "rig," what my family calls a fashion challenged outfit. She pranced around like a proud peacock, making sure Dad noticed.

When all the confusion died down, Dad asked me if I had a night light and I told him that I didn't. Mom said she did, but she reminded him it was *one hundred and sixty miles* away. Ouch! It started all over again. Something about, "the next time," and "when we got in the car," and, "never would have believed." Then Dad asked me for some Tylenol.

One thing that got left behind was Mom's red top to match her black-checked suit (in the hang-up bag). *What a coincidence,* I thought, as I had already planned to give her a brand new red sweater-set that was too long for me. A second coincidence found me buying a red summer sweater the next morning. That night we both looked great when we joined Russell and Dad for dinner.

The same shopping experience that landed me the red sweater must have gotten Mom in the mood to shop after all, because the next thing I knew she was trying on shoes in a boutique near my home. Since Mom wears a hard-to-find size (six-and-a-half slim), the shoe clerk was able to quickly tell us what she had in stock to fit. And wouldn't you know it? Mom got lucky (at Dad's expense). She found a comfy black Birkenstock-type sandal, a soft brown leather kiltie-tie slide, and a dressy bone open-toed heel. Even though she didn't end up with three outfits, she ended up with *three pairs of shoes!* At least her findings were apparel, right? And I forgot to mention she found another pair of bone flats in the same store I found my red sweater.

All this makes me think: When you're traveling and suddenly realize you're missing your luggage, there's only one course of action: adjust, accept, and adapt—then go shopping! And remember, ladies, that's one outfit per day—or, at the very least, one pair of shoes for each day.

Where Am I Going to Lie When My Life Is Over?

D o you ever wonder how different your life might have been "if only"? If only you'd taken that job transfer, finished your MBA, or married your first love? Come to find out, if I'd married a veteran, a certain coupon guarantees me a free burial plot.

I knew I should have married a serviceman way back when. I always thought the military had some fine perks: the PX (Public Exchange—cheap prices and no taxes), free medical and dental care, inexpensive military housing, and a chance to live overseas.

It would have been easy enough to become a military wife. I grew up in Jacksonville, North Carolina, home of Camp Lejeune. Don't say I didn't try. In my early twenties, I spent each Friday night at the New River Air Station Officer's Club, dancing to Steely Dan, Credence Clearwater Revival, and The Doobie Brothers. That's where the drop-dead gorgeous Marine pilots outnumbered us dolled-up, hopeful women ten to one. My girlfriends and I listened to tales of pilots flying CH46's, CH53's, Hueys, and those amazing vertical take-off jets, the Cobras. Other conversations turned to flying formations, squadron names, and tours of duty. In fact, I got to be such an authority on military ranking, that I memorized the insignia on uniforms, starting with Second Lieutenant (one gold bar), all the way up to Lieutenant Colonel (one silver oak leaf).

But it was just not meant to be, my marrying a military officer from a nearby base. Instead, I married a loan officer from a nearby bank. He didn't own a uniform, though he often wore a starched, blue Gant shirt, khaki pants, and Weejuns. He didn't fly a helicopter or a jet, but he darted around town in a reddish-orange, souped-up TransAm. He *did* have a college degree and a good income, and I fell in love with his dry sense of humor and twinkling blue eyes. Russell and I were married happily ever after.

I've often heard that in life, two things—taxes and death—are certain, and you have to *pay* for both of them. I've also heard, "You can't take it with you, but you can't go without it." But since I didn't marry a veteran, I'm not eligible for that dang free plot!

I'm sorry, call me cynical, dubious, or outright suspicious, but I don't buy into this free burial space idea. What's the catch? Now, if this was a discount coupon for say, a Porsche 911 Turbo, I might be interested. At least then, I'd get to drive around town and enjoy the deal while I'm still living. (No cruising down Ocean Boulevard with the aforementioned coupon. No sir, you can't go too far in that burial space—you're sorta stuck!)

Instead, I now cruise around town with Russell often by my side in my Kia Sportage. And in the very end, free burial plot or not, we'll still be together, side by side. It's been a great life and I wouldn't change a thing. Love really does conquer all, with or without coupons—and with or without military privileges.

Oprah Said, "I Feel Duped" (Do What? Do What?)

At the risk of insulting Oprah Winfrey, I must say when I read her quote, "I feel duped," referring to James Frey's not-entirely-true-memoir *A Million Little Pieces*, I imagined a catchy, new pop song. Here are my home-grown lyrics, "I feel duped—doo wap, doo wap. I feel duped—doo wap, doo wap. I feel duped—doo wap, doo wap." Sorry, but the words didn't get any further in my mind. However, I thought back to the late 1960s singing groups The Shirelles, The Dixie Cups, and The Supremes, when my two sisters and I pantomimed their songs while holding a hair brush for a microphone. And though "doo wap, doo wap" was a popular refrain then, it still works today. Or then again, maybe I'd change the refrain to "do what? do what?"

You see, I also feel duped. "Do what?" you say. Let me explain. Over a year ago, my dear friend Rose Rock (yes, Chris Rock's mom) sent Oprah Winfrey a copy of my latest book, my bio, and a personal letter from me. Heck, I felt I owed Oprah a debt of gratitude! I'd heard her advice in her segments "Live Your Best Life," "Remembering Your Spirit," and "Transform Your Life." I'd watched her TV show, read her magazine, bought her books. Plus, I'd seen so many people on her show just like me—ordinary folks struggling with one thing or another: career, finances, love, hurts. I just knew, just absolutely *knew* she would find my situation most interesting. (So would Dr. Phil, but that's another matter.) Heck, Oprah was my mentor, my angel, my role model. And yet…no reply ever came from the Diva of Daytime Talk.

But back to the newspaper quote. Oprah said, "Truth matters." Darned straight it does! And herein, my friends, lays my dilemma (and Oprah's). If she had picked my book *Life Is Short, But It's Wide (In the Southern State of Reality)* for her nationwide book club pick, she most certainly would not have been duped! "Dubbed" perhaps, but not duped. Dubbed insightful, representative, and shrewd to have picked *me* for her book club selection, but certainly not duped.

That's because my memoirs/humor book is one-hundred percent true. I've got the weary, confused, downtrodden, and hopeless to back me up. For instance, my former co-workers at the dental office can attest to the fact that yes, indeed, I got the mayor's mustache caught in my dental hygiene polisher, which nearly killed him and maimed me (emotionally) for life. Myrtle Beach TV show-host Diane DeVaughn Stokes is a witness to another terrible accident, where at Coastal Baseball Field, I got hit in the head, not by a foul ball but by a one-and-a-half-inch roofing screw that was knocked loose by the errant foul ball. (Diane was sitting in front of me.)

My sister remembers well the day in Dilliard's when my own shoes came up missing. A super-savings shopper confessed (after my thorough search) that she found them below the rack of sale shoes and was awaiting a price check. Another witness for Oprah: The dean of a local technical school (where my cake decorating class was being held) can recant the tale of my driving over an orange highway cone in the pot-holed, gravel parking lot on that dark and stormy night, thereby causing the cone to get sucked up under my wheel base. He probably distinctly remembers taking his life into his own hands (amongst thunder and lightening), playing tug of war with that menacing cone.

My husband would swear out an affidavit that yes, it's true I lost my car in the mall parking lot after the movie, during Katie's eighth birthday party. He had half of the birthday guests in his car, and I had the other half. His passengers went on to our home, enjoying ice cream and cake, while I searched and sweated for a solid hour with four frantic kids perched at my heels in the scorching ninety-degree heat. (How was I to know the theatre had two exits?) And the list goes on and on...

Lest you think these are just a few isolated incidences, let me reassure you, *they are not*. I've been called "a magnet for the unusual" and here's further proof. As recently as yesterday, after doing a book signing in Charleston, South Carolina (where, I might add Ms. Winfrey will be speaking in a couple of weeks at $125 a pop—my talk was *free*), I walked into my favorite steakhouse that wasn't there. It's true that I'm not good at navigating and perhaps I wasn't paying close attention. The parking lot seemed a wee bit smaller than before and I also noticed the hostess seated me in a "new area." (I presumed a smoking section was converted to "non smoking"—my preference). And while I'd never been brought a bowl of salsa before *and* the menu had changed, I still had no clue—until the server came forward and said, "How are you, ma'am?" (A typical well-mannered Southern gentleman.)

That's when I blurted out, "Oh! I'm not supposed to be *here!*" Without missing a beat, the waiter cautiously said, "Okay. Now, then. Where are you supposed to be?" I said, "I'm supposed to be at The Longhorn." He continued, "Oh, I see. Are you meeting someone?" "No," I said, "I just wanted to go there."

To make a short story long, I stayed and ordered a salad and a pork tamale. When I finished, I motioned for the server (who kept an eye on me throughout the meal). He said, "There's no charge for your meal today. It was a treat." I stammered. I stuttered. I stumbled. "But, but—" "No," he insisted, saying he hoped I enjoyed the meal and would come back soon.

Y'all, I'd love to go again, with Oprah sitting right beside me, because she'll want to verify these final facts before recommending my book for the All-New Oprah's Book Club!

Keep Your Eyes on the Road, Keep Your Hands on the Wheel

Do you remember that old song, "Keep Your Eyes on the Road, Keep Your Hands on the Wheel"? Well, if you're not a baby boomer like me, you may not remember it, but those words were never truer than now.

In a recent article in *USA Today* entitled, "Americans Driving to Distraction," Debbie Howlett addresses a new concern about folks driving and doing a multitude of tasks at the same time. This article lists several culprits. For instance, talking on the cellphone, eating a burger, and adjusting the radio knob. But the shocker was "[drivers] reading the newspaper as they drive down I-95." How could anyone possibly do that? (I wonder if those drivers are reading *USA Today?* Hmm...) I can think of other culprits—namely, what about those prissy women who apply mascara while driving? That is just not smart. A woman driving next to me appeared to be doing this very thing recently. But then I noticed a grimace come across her face. Well, no wonder. Danged if she wasn't plucking her brows. Come on! That driver needs a ticket and a new brain to go along with it.

Anyway, a New Jersey Assemblyman named Doug Fisher proposed a ban last spring on this so-called "distracted driving." Of course, the deejays on the radio had a ball with the very idea, even calling it DWE for "driving while eating" and "the ham-sandwich law." However, Fisher only got part of his wish, banning cellphone use only, just like New York did in 2001. The new law is effective in New Jersey in July, and a similar law begins the same month in Washington, D.C.

It's probably a good idea—at least about banning cellphones. But my family is doomed if they pass the "ham-sandwich law." Oh, don't worry, I never eat while driving—unless you count Listerine breath strips. And Russell doesn't eat while driving either—unless we are going out of town. Even then, he doesn't eat, he just chews. That's because I feed him. Yes, it sounds sick. I'll pinch off a piece of burger and plop it in his mouth, or sit back and throw a fry at him, as if he's a hungry puppy. I'm getting pretty good at sending food and he's getting pretty good at receiving it. Both hands stay on the steering wheel, so technically, that is not eating. The biggest risk he ever faces is dripping mayonnaise down his $74 Tommy Hilfiger slacks and then paying the $6 dry cleaning fee.

You might wonder just how far the legislature could go with this anti-distraction thing. The scary part is I'm afraid Russell would be charged just because he is sitting beside me and he says *I'm* a distraction, talking a mile a minute. It starts out like this, "Honey, did I tell you we got our personal property tax statement today, and it's more than doubled? How come?" A minute passes by and I've read two more exit signs. Then I get bored and say, "When are we going on a cruise? It's been over two years now and I'm *reeeeady.*" Next, I'll read the newspaper a little while (I'm allowed, since I'm not driving) and I'll tell him some hard-to-believe story, like the one about the grandmother who gave birth to her own grandchildren.

About that time he takes a deep breath and makes a face like his head might be starting to hurt, using both hands to grip the hair on his head. Oops! Better get those hands back on the steering wheel. That's when I tell Russell if he's looking for peace and quiet, he really should stay home. But I quickly add, "And give me the charge card, so I can go to the new mall."

This same article also said that ten states—that's a lot—last year considered legislation that would try to curb distracting driving habits. Most bills would allow police to ticket an inattentive driver. Now, this is the clincher: The police can decide what constitutes inattentive behavior. Well, there you go. Half of our tourists (and some of our local drivers) will be sitting on the side of the road, blue lights flashing behind them. I can hear it now. "Officer, I didn't mean for my van to weave. It's just that I got distracted by that three-by-four-foot map that I was holding. You see, Ethel here, and I, are from West Virginia and we're just trying to locate the Alabama Theatre. Is it in Alabama?" Folks, we are in big trouble if inattentive drivers will get ticketed in South Carolina, because you must admit that's pretty much everybody. I think it would be a lot easier to just give out rewards for those who *are* paying attention. Y'know?

This is the deal: A study at the University of Utah is trying to prove that the cellphone users are a bigger threat than drunken drivers. This phenomenon is called "inattentional blindness." I promise that is the term, but for the life of me, my brain can't comprehend such gibberish. In the test, using a driving simulator (a what?), drivers are given vodka and orange juice (I wonder if it's during happy hour) until they exceeded a blood-alcohol level of 0.08%, the legal limit for most states. These folks had fewer accidents and quicker reaction times while they were legally drunk than when sober and talking on a cellphone. Oh, that's just great. Not!

When the final results are posted, I'm afraid every Tom, Dick, and Harry will hit the bar at quitting time, get snockered on screwdrivers, forget to call their spouses/significant other(s) and then realize once they're behind the wheel, they can't call home. 'Cause one thing's for sure, they best not pick up that cellphone once they start driving.

Opening Impossible Packages (Plissors to the Rescue!)

I was talking to my mom recently when I asked if she liked the CD I'd given her for Christmas. "Well, ah, no, not yet," she answered. "What do you mean?" I asked. She said after battling the cover, in which the flimsy cellophane stuck like glue to her fingers, another problem arose: the narrow sticky sealing tape band wouldn't budge.

I knew exactly what she meant. The last time I tried to open a new CD I was driving and fiddling with the bag, the receipt, and the CD (my bad). Lucky for me, I keep a pair of scissors in the glove compartment. Unlucky for my car, I almost poked a hole in the upholstery. (Add that to your list of what not to do while driving: talking on a cellphone, applying make-up or pantyhose {just kidding}, and opening those #$%!* CD packages.)

One more cellophane-and-cardboard death trap is the VCR tape packaging. Yes, we Ipocks still have a VCR—but in the essence of fairness, and so we don't sound like we're living in a time warp, Russell did buy a DVD player recently. Since my TV recordings are rarely planned (it's not like I'm sitting around making daily flow charts), when I do need to record, the actual show has likely already begun. It goes like this: "Oh my gosh! 'Grey's Anatomy' [my current favorite show] is on," whereupon Russell rolls his eyes and says, "So? Go watch it!" "No, "I tell him, "I'm busy now. I want to watch it later." After Russell sees that I mean business, and being the kind-hearted guy that he is, he runs around trying to aid and abet me, joining in the search for a new (unused) tape.

"Aha! I've got it!" At this point, the show has progressed to the first commercial. I sigh. Suddenly, Russell screams in agony. I stare at him. "What?" I ask. "I can't get the package open," he cries. With chewed-down-to-the-nub fingernails and large hands, he appears to be all thumbs. The menacing black box flies up in the air and crashes to the floor. But you guessed it, still intact.

Recently I got a shock when I came home from the grocery store and noticed my dishwasher detergent bottle has now copied those annoying childproof medicine caps. Frustration ensues when I read the latest directions: "Squeeze cap sides while unscrewing." *Fuhgedaboutit!* I can squeeze or unscrew, but I can't do both at once. The cap also reads, "Close tight." Oh, don't worry, I think the cap will remain closed because *I can't get it open in the first place!* Whether it's from arthritis, bursitis, or tendonitis, I can't maneuver this feat. On a second try, with sore hand and hurt feelings, I manage to remove it, but in doing so, I shake the bottle, sending the lemony glutinous mixture flying straight out in one fat spurt, landing on the floor.

Well, all this package-opening insanity is nothing compared to buying (opening) my newest Sony Walkman that I use at the gym. It seems a new packaging device sucks out all the air out between the cardboard and the steel-hard clear plastic. And there are no instructions telling us how we are supposed to attack and destroy this packaging that's so tough not even a truck rolling over it will dent it. Not so much as a mention of "Open here, you fool, if you can." *As if it were possible.* So you push, prod, and pray. Nothing. Then you stomp on it, scream at it, and spin it like a Frisbee. Nothing.

It seems to me that all of this idiotic "you can't get to me" protective coating has indeed finally gotten to me—but I don't give up easy, and I do have a solution that I've invented in my mind's eye. "Plissors." It's a cross between a pair of pliers and a pair of scissors. Strong enough to open any package by pulling apart the steel-like plastic from the super-duper thick cardboard, and yet sharp enough to cut through any clingy cellophane or sticky sealing tape. But wait! There's more! As an added bonus, these plissors would come with a bonus gift: a handy-dandy attachment that pops off those childproof caps with a squeeze and a turn, all by itself. Any schemers out there looking for a get-rich-quick and much needed invention? These ideas I've just outlined should help.

Meanwhile, why doesn't someone develop a task force to study and implement packaging standards? Let's simplify opening things for us average, well-educated, but non-engineering consumers! Or else, does anyone know a good patent lawyer for my plissors?

When Shopping for Shoes, Mine Disappeared

I'm fairly good, though not great, at keeping up with my things, be it my business or social calendar or matters of a personal nature such as my wardrobe, hair and nail appointments, and health care matters. Though I'm not a control freak *per se*, I admit to being a little compulsive. For instance, I like to store my shoes in their original boxes. I like my blinds to be turned up to filter out bright morning light. And I always keep my cordless phone within arm's reach. (You never know when the "Oprah" show might call!)

But imagine how out of control I felt (not to mention helpless), when my shoes recently disappeared on a shopping trip out of town. Some people say that we control our own destiny, but I was just trying to keep up with my shoes.

Speaking of shoes, anybody that knows me knows I love them. As I've mentioned before, this obsession dates back to my teenage days working at our family business. Still, I've cut back some over the last few years, getting by with perhaps six (instead of sixteen) purchases a year.

On a recent trip out of town, my party of five discovered our restaurant wait would be over an hour. What else could we do but shop at the nearest mall? My sister Nancy headed for ladies clothing, my husband, Russell, and nephew Huck headed to the sporting goods store, and my friend Jennifer and I headed for the shoe department. While there, I discovered several racks of "too good to be true" bargains. Imagine my delight to find many $99 shoes slashed to $9.99. I never knew that moving a decimal could feel so good! I was in Cinderella heaven.

After my third "Wow!" from yet another successful shoe selection, Jennifer seemed worried. She grabbed my arm and pointed to her watch, saying, "We're going to be late for dinner. We've got five minutes to make it to the restaurant!" I told Jennifer to hold on, that

I was waiting for a missing shoebox. This mishap didn't surprise me because the store, crawling with hungry bargain hunters, was a mess. Mismatched pairs, overturned boxes, and shoes were strewn all over the floor. "Don't worry about the silly box," Jennifer insisted.

"But I like to keep my shoes organized in boxes," I whined. Jennifer then gave me that defiant Aunt Esther-look from "Sanford and Son," almost hitting me with her pocketbook.

"All right," I pouted, barefooted and frowning, preparing to pay for three pairs (minus one box) and rush over to the Macaroni Grill.

But when I went to slip on my Born mules that I'd worn into the store, they were nowhere to be found. Bewildered, I searched frantically through the racks of size six through eight. That was a large range I realize, but you know my philosophy—if they're on sale and they look good, buy them, regardless. Too small? Shoot, just cram your foot into those suckers, they'll stretch eventually. Too big? No problem, just insert a pair of innersoles. But do not let that bargain go, girrrrll! It's a woman's prerogative.

My search was in vain. My shoes had vanished. I'm no detective, but it appeared to me that the shoes I'd walked in with had gotten up and walked out—by themselves.

Two ladies, who were sitting nearby, trying on sale shoes, saw this commotion. I told them what had happened, describing my missing shoes (which were barely two weeks old and looked new).

"Those were yours?" a lady exclaimed. "I didn't know that. I wanted them. The clerk is getting a price check for me right now!"

My eyes bugged out. I couldn't speak. I ran towards the stock room, almost knocking down the lady who came through the door. She rushed past me, holding my shoes close to her chest. I shouted to her, "Those are mine!"

"No, I'm sorry. These are for another customer," she said, clutching the shoes even tighter and pointing to the lady waiting for the price. Was it just me or did her attitude imply she was there first? I then told the clerk my story. (Good thing I wasn't shopping for a bathing suit.)

About this time, my cellphone rang and Russell, said, "Where are you? We're late for dinner." "I'm retrieving my shoes." I said.

There was something wrong with this evening. First we strolled about for an hour while waiting for dinner, then we rushed around the last five minutes and hurried to the restaurant.

So once again, the universe sent me a "this could only happen to you" message. Diane DeVaughn Stokes commented on this when she recently interviewed me for her television show "Southern Style." After having read my book *Life Is Short, But It's Wide*, she asked why all these paranormal things happened to me, saying I was a magnet. She may be right—but I'm starting to feel like an out of control magnet!

I've been thinking about all this. On the one hand, my life sure would be simpler if I'd never burned (as in "Fire!") a Thanksgiving turkey, ordered business cards before I actually had a business, dyed my hair burgundy, or yanked out half the mayor's mustache with my dental hygiene polisher. It's also true that some days I wonder if I should even leave the house. This apparent Murphy's Law thing can make you rather paranoid. No, that's silly. I don't believe staying inside would put a negative charge on my so-called magnet. Why, just look at that garbage disposal I killed with ten pounds of dry grits. I never even left the house that day…

Living in the Southern State of Reality

You know, it's hard—no, make that impossible—for me to imagine *not* living at the beach in South Carolina. In fact, the good Lord willing and the creek don't rise, I plan always to live on the coast. To the uninitiated, living "at the beach" (Pawleys Island, in my case) has some real perks. Things like clean air and balmy breezes (and almost never any snow—hallelujah!), winding dirt roads just begging to be traveled, a camera with black-and-white film ready to capture the beauty, a dozen or two pelicans flying overhead, and yes, definitely sand in my shoes (and even more in my trunk). And did I mention beach/shagging music?

In nine years of living at Pawleys, six strange occurrences come to mind. Oddly, in living ten years previous to that in Myrtle Beach, nothing uncanny ever happened. I often say it's as if a curtain drops somewhere around Murrells Inlet (midway between both towns) and there's a change in the air. Life down here in the Lowcountry takes on a whole new persona. Don't get me wrong, some of my best friends live in Myrtle Beach proper and it's a lovely town—but it doesn't have the same ambience.

Of those six things, some are hilarious. Some are preposterous and some are spine tingling. Every one of these scenarios actually happened right smack dab at the Pawleys Island North Causeway.

To begin with, the Fourth of July is probably our biggest holiday; it's when this next story took place. That's also when we're always packed with happy tourists and locals alike, all celebrating.

One time, Katie and I were planning to lay out in the sun. After circling the northern-most part of the island a few times, we found a parking space. The same dilemma was repeated when we searched for a spot to place our chairs. We hadn't been sitting there five minutes when this handsome, preppy, young guy walked over and said, "Hello, ladies. Let me ask you something." We listened because we were very interested. He asked, "Do you see my friend over there?" We looked up and another cutie pie was waving, coy-like. Ha, I thought, this can't be a pick-up, but I sure was flattered. We let him continue. "Do you think he plays horseshoes well?" We shrugged our shoulders. How would we know? "Well," he said, "let me just tell you. He's awful! He can't play well at all. So considering the fact that you are sitting right where we are playing the game, you might want to move." Then he winked and sauntered off. I could've died! We tried to act cool as we nonchalantly hoisted up our bags and zig-zagged our chairs to a new spot, turning away from the horseshoe throwers in order to mask our red, embarrassed faces.

One day in January, Katie and I decided to go for a walk. As I recall, it was cold, but not freezing like a normal winter day. We noticed when we left our house that it was foggy. Less than a mile later when we hit the sand, the air itself was downright eerie. It reminded me of one of those movies where they pump out fog from a fog machine—so thick, as my mama would say, that you couldn't stir it with a stick. Katie and I kidded with each other not to walk too far apart or we might lose each other. And yet, it was beautiful. Mystical. You couldn't *not* want to witness it. I know that stretch of beach like the back of my hand—and yet, I couldn't find our car when we were ready to leave. We had to walk up and inspect each cottage in order to get our bearings, in respect to the parking lot. At the end of our forty-five-minute walk, we both giggled like little girls when seeing each other's wet hair and skin, so much dew had fallen upon us.

Then there was the time I was walking just after dinner one night in late summer. The sun was beginning to set and the air was perfectly still. Suddenly I came upon a big, burly man wearing a bathing suit with a cigar hanging out of his mouth; he had just reeled in a humongous flounder. This was just south of the Pawleys Island pier, where he was surf fishing. I stopped to get a better look and congratulate him. He laughed, nodded his head appreciatively, and then asked me a surprising question. "Would you like to take it home?" I was so shocked all I could get out was, "Oh, noooooooo, thank you." I mean, think about it. How was I supposed to drag home a *live* (though not for long), slimy, squirmy flounder—tie it to my shoe?—and me being a quarter of a mile from my car? I don't think so! Imagine those fish eyes staring me down while I drove. And anyway, I don't even know how to clean fish. (Neither did the tourist-fisherman, he confessed.) To this day, my friends chide me about "the big one that got away."

When my sister Nancy was visiting from Raleigh one time, we walked on the same stretch of beach. It was a sunny day and people were out just having fun. Children were digging trenches, families were playing bocce, and others were just lying out in chairs, enjoying a good beach read, getting a suntan. I spotted two young boys playing Frisbee and didn't think much of it. That is, until…in a surreal, slow motion sort of way, the Frisbee left the hand of one of them and I watched it moving towards Nancy and me. I opened my mouth in disbelief, as the disk spun closer, closer. I continued walking, thinking, "Nah, it won't hit us." Well it did! Not only did the Frisbee hit me, but *where* it hit me was horrific—under my left knee exactly where I have a small scar from the time when I was a child and climbed up and then fell off a chest of drawers, resulting in stitches. Ouch! And get this, the guy didn't even say he was sorry. I thought to myself he sure was sorry!

Another occurrence that happened at the beach was when I locked my keys in the car. Maybe it happened because I was driving Russell's car while mine was being tuned up. I'd no more slammed the door when I realized it. I immediately went to the first cottage I saw and asked to use a phone. Here I am, a stranger asking another stranger for the use of his phone. I guess I didn't look too dangerous, so this kind man consented. Well, since the phone had a "block" on it, no calls could be made to Myrtle Beach (where Russell works). Not to worry. That was when I called a friend who in turned called Russell at work. Just like clockwork, at the end of my forty-five minute walk, Russell appeared. Pretty lucky, wasn't I?

Finally, I've met people of different occupations on the beach, sometimes in the midst of their work, sometimes in the midst of their play, and once in the midst of their wedding. (I even got invited to a wedding in front of a cottage once.) I recently met a beautiful and talented artist from Columbia who was getting married later that month. She was painting in oil the Sea View Inn and I was just enthralled. We exchanged names and she painted my name on her canvas. Isn't that something? No paper, no pen, no problem! She told me an interesting anecdote that I just have to share, about her mother finding an injured chicken on the side of the road, picking it up, and trying to carry it to a vet (which was Amanda's fiancé, actually), but the chicken never made it there. That was because her mom first made a stop at the nursing home in Georgetown to visit Amanda's grandmother. When she returned, the chicken, as her mom said, "Was all puffed up, got all haughty, and then flew away." Is that a story or what?

Well, there you have it. Pelicans, flounder, chickens. This place is not only home, it's entertainment. If those reality shows in New York and California think they are depicting real life, I've got this to tell them: In South Carolina, we are *living* in the Southern State of Reality! Come on down to the Lowcountry, and I'll show you a slice of life that most people couldn't imagine. And you know what? I absolutely love it.

"The Blog" Is "The Blah"

Recently my webmaster, Ron, and I decided to update my Web site. After all, the site is two years old and it's time. Ron and I have been discussing ways to streamline the headings, make it easier to read, condense the verbiage, and add some zip—vibrant colors, varied fonts, artsy borders. I've literally spent days poring over other Web sites for ideas, then e-mailing Ron, then meeting with him—all with the goal of making the site more attractive and user-friendly. Along these lines, we've added a photo gallery, which will serve as a snapshot, if you will, of what's going on around here.

In addition, Ron has strongly encouraged me to start writing in a blog. Though I think most computer users know what a blog is, I'll spell it out anyway. Blog is short for "Web log," thus take the "b" from "web" and attach it to "log," then repeat after me. "Blog." Ron told me this was the most popular trend in Computerville these days, reassuring me with, "Everybody's doing it." But just as my sweet-but-firm Mama used to say to me way back in the 1960s, I asked Ron if everybody was sticking their hand in a fan, would he? Hmmmm? He just arched one eyebrow and shook that silly computer mouse at me.

In a solid month, I've only written two blog entries. Hey, I'm trying, but it's difficult! I seem to be drawing a blank on this new form of communication. Yeah, I know, Russell tells everyone I'm never at a loss for words. I tell him it's called being an extrovert, but no, he says, it's called being annoying. What do men know? And though I've been writing in several genres on a computer for over fifteen years, it seems to me that writing in a blog is different, very different—a "scripted life," you might say.

Also, this freeing venue might tempt one to record information much too personal. At the other extreme, whatever isn't personal seems mundane. Is there nothing in between? It's one thing to announce we will soon be grandparents; it's another thing entirely to announce to the world that I survived that horrid root canal or that

I saved $6.78 by simply using my PFC card at the local Piggly Wiggly. Who really cares?

The way I see it, a blog is similar to a reality TV show—only nobody's getting paid and no one's appearing on a TV screen. Plus it's not "live" and it can be edited, which is *a good thing, Martha.* Well, I guess if there are people hard up enough to watch those nutty reality TV shows such as "Survivor," "Extreme Makeover," and "The Bachelor" (Kelly's fave, go figure), then maybe that's the same folks who will be reading my blog.

I remain skeptical, still not believing anyone would want to read about my boring life. Wait a minute—that's it! If I can make my life more exciting, then my blog will be more exciting! Talk about justifying a means to an end. A three-week jaunt throughout Europe would give me plenty to blog about. Quick, I better book my flight before I chicken out.

There's only one thing holding me back. Uh huh, you guessed it. Oscar (a.k.a. Russell). Maybe I better run these plans by him first. I can see it now. After he hems and haws, throws a conniption fit, takes the passive/aggressive route, then jolts me back to reality with a lecture about "common sense, budget, and practicality," I'll have more than enough to fill a page in my blog.

Eenie, Meanie, Miney, Mo!

C*hoices.* That's a word (and concept) I'd rather avoid. In fact, I've always hated making decisions. Friends and family can tell you that I am the *Queen of Indecisiveness,* so I guess that makes me choice-challenged.

But all that changed for me recently, putting things in perspective, when I saw what huge choices my friend Linda was forced to make regarding her car. Linda bought a 1984 gray Mercedes station wagon—an older, classic, dependable, and solid car—four years ago. The reason she picked this car was because it was unique and not a part of the SUV, convertible sports car, or luxury sedan craze. What minor problems she's experienced over the years—such as the time her family had two wrecks in one day (Linda backed into the fence and then her daughter backed into Linda's car)—she chose not to repair, saying she'd rather sink her money into more important things. Things like a new couch, her daughter's wedding, or a trip to San Francisco.

But lately, Linda's had major things to go wrong with the car, and they've happened all at once. For starters, after her daughter got married, Linda offered to dog-sit while the honeymooners went away. One afternoon with Spud in tow, Linda popped into a store. She left the windows slightly cracked (for ventilation), and the keys in the ignition. When she returned to her car, an odd thing happened. She was locked out! Spud had pushed down all four buttons, smudging the windows with his paw prints.

Linda called her husband, who brought her an extra key. When she opened the car door, she was met with flying red feathers, which eventually fell to the navy leather interior, the dash, and the floorboard. Evidently Spud had found the feather duster inside and must have fought the thing, using his teeth and paws as he gnashed and thrashed about, tearing it to shreds. Upon further inspection, Linda noticed that Spud had chewed a quarter-sized-hole through the leather seat. That was bad enough, but when Linda reached for her seatbelt, she saw it was considerably shorter than before. Spud had gnawed it in half!

Now picture this. Linda is driving down the road with red feathers flying in her hair, her face, landing in her opened (as in "shocked") mouth, unable to see because of the dirty windshield, with her body sliding uncontrollably across the seat (thanks to no seatbelt). All this time, frisky Spud is jumping around barking, panting, and wagging his tail. Larry asked her later if they should consider buying a new car. She told him no, the choice was simple. She wanted to keep the car, but she was glad she didn't have to keep the dog. (She did get the seatbelt repaired.)

Linda called me recently and asked me to go to lunch. By then, she'd cleaned up the car and things were semi-back to normal—with one exception. The turn signals quit working. We were on our way to lunch when she explained this, saying she now used hand signals when turning, but it was so hot that day she didn't want to roll down the window. As we were ready to turn into the restaurant, a policeman came up behind us. I said, "What are you going to do, you'll get a ticket if you turn with no signal?" Linda answered, "Drive to Florida, I guess." Luckily, the officer turned and so did we. (A couple of fuses fixed the problem later on.)

Two weeks later we were riding down the road when I said, "So, how's your car doing?" Believe me, it's become a hot topic of conversation. She recounted how the driver's window had fallen: She pushed the button and the window got stuck halfway. Then her daughter borrowed the car to move some furniture. When she and her husband tried to roll it down, it made a strange noise, then a thud, as it fell to the bottom of the track. It was raining, so they wedged an umbrella at the window to keep dry. (The window got repaired immediately.)

Linda went on to say that the air conditioner had broken, but it had also been fixed. It seems she found a mechanic who specialized in foreign car repair and she asked him if he thought the car was worth repairing. Not only did he think it was worth repairing, he told her she should *never, ever sell it*. That's how special he thought her Mercedes was. (He gets credit for that decision.) So, she left it to be repaired. When she picked the car up, he said he had good news and bad news. The good news was he had cold air coming out of the front vents. The bad news was the cold air was also coming out of the dash. Linda asked him could that be fixed as well. He said yes, but it would cost an extra $200 to take the entire dash out. Or, he explained, she could buy one of those draft dodgers that people place inside the doors of their home to keep cold air out.

As decisive and determined as Linda had been to that point, she said this was the last straw. Frantically, she called her husband and told him that she couldn't take it anymore, saying she wanted to keep the car, but she absolutely was not driving around with a stuffed snake jammed into her dashboard. Larry said they should definitely get it fixed, reasoning that the repair bill would cost less than a new car payment. The last time we spoke, Linda said the car was running fine. But I had a headache just thinking about what she'd been through.

I decided there has got to be a better way. I've now devised an easy method for making choices in the future. Whether I'm choosing seafood or beef for dinner, wearing black or white to a party, or vacationing in the Outer Banks or Cozumel, I've got this thing whipped. I'll simply narrow my choices, use common sense, and of course, my deductive powers of reasoning—then I'll say, "Eenie, meanie, miney, mo." Maybe Linda should try that too.

CHAPTER 7
Family Zoo and Pesky Relatives

Today's Grandmothers: Daring Divas and Cool Chicks

No doubt about it, more and more, we grandmothers aren't what we used to be. It's a fact that we maintain busier lifestyles, have healthier bodies, and live longer lives than our grandmothers before us. We're as likely to be found in the gym as the grocery store, or the boardroom as the bedroom. Instead of sewing, many of us are surfing the Web *and* surfing in the ocean. And we're often found building nest eggs as well as building homes. We're also running marathons and running for public office. It's a far cry from the 1950s and '60s when I think back to my grandmothers' lives.

I remember my grandmother Julia Margaret—a Southern belle with a name to prove it—wearing her signature housedress, sitting there crocheting antimacassars (doilies for arm rests), baby blankets, and booties. By contrast, I wear my bathing suit to the beach and jump waves with my four-year-old granddaughter Madison, then build sandcastles. My grandmother wore her hair gray, short, and permed. I wear my hair blonde, bobbed, and bouncy. My grandmother loved to eat collards. I love to eat calamari. My grandmother once drove twelve miles to tour The Tryon Palace (the governor's mansion in New Bern, North Carolina—the state's original capital before Raleigh). I flew twelve-hundred miles to tour the Mayan ruins in Cancun. My grandmother smoked like a freight train. I walk and jog like a speeding train.

In contrast, I likely had more in common with Grandmother Pinky ("Granny Go-Go"). We both loved beautiful clothes, sporty red fingernails, taking trips, and making people laugh. Granny also crocheted, but I think she loved cooking more. She also enjoyed canning and pickling, and she always set an inviting supper table. But as she got older and her arthritis got worse, she took on this certain waddling gait that proved to the world she was hurting. She let her hair go gray and started wearing old lady shoes. Flip-flops are still my shoe of choice. It's quite a contrast—their lives and mine. They were "old" when they were still young (my current age), and I'm—well, just starting life, it seems.

I reflected upon this a while back when Russell announced that we were eligible for AARP membership. I scoffed at the idea. He couldn't understand my reluctance, but I insisted that we weren't in that age category and we weren't retired—the two requirements I thought AARP listed. Well, I was wrong on both accounts. He explained that you only have to be fifty years old (checkmark) and not retired (checkmark, again); the benefits include receiving their magazine and discounts for various products and services. "Yeah, yeah, whatever," I said, unconvinced. He went ahead and signed us both up. The day it arrived in the mail, Russell handed me my red and white card with the AARP emblem, with a wink in his eye. I sheepishly slipped it into a dresser drawer rather than my wallet, still refusing to consider myself a member of an "old folk's club." Well, ha! The joke was on me.

A few days later, the *AARP Magazine* arrived and I was flabbergasted! With cover models like Bill Cosby, Cybill Shepherd, and Billy Crystal, I am both impressed and intrigued. I sat down and read it cover-to-cover that day. It turns out this slick, glossy publication is colossal, chic, and cool! While it's not *Cosmo*, it does have some very interesting articles with subjects including: how to avoid being ripped off with major purchases, solving health care issues, boosting your brain power, planning and attending reunions, building wealth for retirement, and sharing grandparent confessions. The magazine not only has a sense of humor with its playful and light-hearted look at us aging baby boomers, but it is also realistic and encouraging with its enlightening interviews showing milestones and triumphs, which scream out to the reader, "You can do it, too!"

And just as Russell says (don't you hate it when he's right?), now

I find that being a member of AARP does indeed offer us some pretty significant discounts. Just this week I planned a vacation at a beach resort. When I asked the reservationist on the phone if they accept AARP, she proudly said, "Yes ma'am! You get a 10% discount." See there, I saved a whopping $60 by using my card. I then went straight to that dresser drawer, and since I'm now a confirmed (and accepting) member, I slipped the card into my wallet.

I've heard folks say that age is only a number and I agree. In fact, I often say that I would not go back to being thirty—oh sure, maybe I'd like that body, but then again, my guess is that I'm healthier now. And I wouldn't trade the wisdom and knowledge I have gained over the years, even considering the School of Hard Knocks I've sometimes attended, for anything in the world. This Grammy Annie (Madison's name for me) is quite happy, thank you very much! And I love the ability of having so many choices at this stage in my life. Whether traveling, accepting a new writing assignment, signing up for classes, or playing with my granddaughter, I'm looking forward to the next fifty some years!

Hand-Me-Down Clothes:
Tacky for Teens,
But Awesome for Adults

When I was growing up, most of my clothes consisted of hand-me-downs. Having two older sisters ensured that my wardrobe, though ample, would consist of worn, older, and dated pieces. I knew not to complain or else that parental speech of "be thankful for what you have" would be given for the umpteenth time. It wasn't so much the guilt, embarrassment, or humiliation that got to me during those moments. It was the long, drawn-out repetitive message that would lead into a series of other questions, like "Have you cleaned your room?" "Done your homework?" "Contributed to the Presidential Election Campaign?" I swore when I grew up I would never repeat those rotten clichés to my children. I also swore I'd never again wear hand-me-downs. Not no way. Not no how. Not ever. And I didn't—at least, not for thirty-some years.

But then one Christmas, Katie (now twenty-one) got this gorgeous multi-colored hand-knitted ski sweater from The Gap as a present. I said, "Cute! Can I wear it sometime?" I forgot about it until one day, a couple of years later, I was in her closet looking for a book and caught a glimpse of that old ski sweater. I tried it on and simply loved it.

Further searching in that same closet yielded discoveries better than consignment shop bargains. I found black stretch pants, a three-quarter length stretchy top, even a sexy black party dress and other items. The black slacks looked great with my pink structured jacket. The top looked awesome with my Levi jeans. And when I wore the sexy black dress to a cocktail party, I heard many compliments. At one point, I asked Katie exactly what she was wearing at college since it appeared most of her clothes were here—but she is a minimalist to a fault, and said she didn't need them all. Me, on the other hand, ha! I was so elated to have a new wardrobe that I searched Katie's closet even closer, hanger by hanger, grabbing all I could find. Before long, I added a jacket, a belt, and a cute tee shirt. And though I swore I'd never wear hand-me-downs again, I was doing so—and both happy and grateful for them.

A funny thing happened recently. When celebrating my best friend, Carolyn's, birthday, several folks came by and picked me up in her SUV on the way to dinner. Her daughter Emily was riding along and said, "Miss Ann, I love that sweater. Several of my friends have it. I almost bought it a few years ago at The Gap." Well. My secret was out. It was a teenager's sweater. It was old. And it was a hand-me-down. Instinctively I responded, "Yeah. This used to belong to Katie."

Then, when I told Carolyn about how much I loved her new jean jacket, she said, "Oh! It's not new. It's a hand-me-down from Suzanne" (her other daughter). I giggled. "You too?" It turns out that we've both increased our wardrobes considerably with various things from scarves to tops to shirts. But one thing neither of us can share with our daughters (we each have two) are shoes, unfortunately. I don't know how it can be that Carolyn and I both wear size seven-and-a-half shoes and our daughters wear size nine.

I've determined that hand-me-downs aren't so bad after all. Now when Katie buys something new, I find myself looking forward to the day she might leave it behind. This new method of acquiring clothes has many advantages: I don't have to find a dressing room to try it on, wonder how I'm going to pay for it, or dread Russell fussing at me for buying "more things that [I] don't need." When we're teens, we think hand-me-downs are tacky. But when we're adults, we think they're awesome! Another one of life's mysteries.

Family Competition: In Search of the Great, White Teeth

When I recently got my teeth cleaned, I mentioned to the dental hygienist that my teeth aren't as white as they used to be. I'm sure she thought, *What you do expect? With age, things deteriorate—and that includes teeth, bones, and mental aptitude.* But lucky for me, she suggested I try tooth whitening strips, which as it happened, she could sell me. I bought them right then and there because: A) they were prescription strength (stronger than store-bought), B) I'm an impulse shopper and, C) I'm a sucker for a new gadget. I've now begun this high-tech, thoroughly amazing feat: bleaching my teeth with hydrogen peroxide. The theory behind the process is really kind of cool—no pain, much gain, and it's fairly inexpensive.

In truth, the harsh reality hit me last night as I applied the first strip. Since I hate to read directions, I didn't. Instead, I thought, *How complicated could this be? It's not like something could go wrong.* But it did. I tore open the foil packet and there were the strips: one for the upper jaw and one for the lower jaw. I set to work, applying the first strip to my upper teeth. It was impossible. That hard plastic would not bend. Plus, it hurt! It gouged my gingiva (that's "gums" in layman's terms—I used to be a dental hygienist until I got the mayor's mustache caught in my tooth polisher, which gave him a permanent twitch and ended his political career).

The inflexible strips made me think that there had to be a better way! I removed the hard, clear strip for inspection, and realized the problem: I was holding the backing to the strip. Geez, I'm almost too embarrassed to admit my mistake—but if I didn't, there would be no story to tell. Next, I applied the flexible, sticky, coated strip, one on top and one on bottom. The next thirty minutes seemed like thirty hours.

Here's the worst part. During that time, I couldn't talk (not even to myself!). I never realized how much I do talk to myself, until then.

Things like, *Go to the bank in the morning. Did I call Kelly? What time are we supposed to meet Sharon and Browney for dinner?* Since Russell wasn't around (out of town on business), I wasn't tempted to talk to him. In fact, I waited until 11 p.m. to apply the strips, knowing he wouldn't call that late.

After my faux pas, I decided maybe I *had* better read the instructions. What if it stated something like, "Do not apply on an empty stomach"—yeah, right, like anyone would do that. Heck, it's hard enough applying them to your *teeth*. So, I pulled out the booklet and began reading. However, all I saw were words written in Spanish. I realize that the Spanish language is gaining in popularity in our country, but I must say: If instructions are going to be printed in Spanish, we need an interpretive dictionary to go along with them. I skimmed several pages, becoming more confused with each new paragraph. Then it dawned on me. *Turn the booklet over.* You know how the Spiegel catalog starts out with furniture or whatever, and then, *voila!* you must *flip the book* to go to the cover for clothes. Well, the instructions booklet was like that.

Today's application, number two, wasn't much better. The top strip broke into three pieces. I had to dab-dab-dab it to keep it in place. Then I noticed the expiration date was twenty days away and this is a twenty-one-day program. Hmmm…

Some people may think I'm whitening my teeth for vanity reasons, and maybe I am. But I also like trying new things, especially for health reasons. It's also true that I'm competitive. Ever since Russell used the strips a month ago, I was tempted to see what success I could achieve (which turned out to be excellent).

You see, Russell made two crucial mistakes, in my opinion, in that he didn't get his teeth cleaned first and he bought non-prescription strips at the drugstore. I told him this before he began the trial, but you know men. You can't tell them anything. I plan to rehash this story again—reminding him to call the dentist—when he returns from Atlanta, as I smile ever so brightly, flashing my pearly whites!

Mama Is Styling in Her Colorful Hibiscus Capris

I read recently that the iconic hibiscus flower is the hottest fashion item going these days, and that you can now find this beautiful state flower of Hawaii in all kinds of places: swimsuits, skirts, dresses, sportswear, and even water bottles. (Living at the beach, I know this to be true because I see this same hibiscus pattern on beach towels, chairs, and umbrellas.) But when I finished reading that article mentioning this savvy trend, I said, "Hush my mouth! Don't my mama know it!" As I tossed the newspaper into the recycle bin, I thought back to my dear, sweet Mama and a recent visit I'd made to her home, where she modeled her very own brand new pair of hibiscus capris.

Let me back up and say that no one would consider Mama a "flashy" dresser. Even now her closet is mostly full of black, khaki, brown, and navy—dignified, though subdued—with just a small sprinkling of red for when she's feeling spunky. Still, Mama has always had a flair for style, even if it didn't include bright psychedelic colors. Now, me? Well, that's a whole other story. The brighter the better! On my parents' fiftieth wedding anniversary (ten years ago) I wore this darling Carole Little outfit with tight black "fruity patterned" leggings and a totally precious oversized black top (remember that hideous wacky style that flattered *no one?*). The size XL top, which could wrap around me twice, featured eye-popping bold embroidered watermelon, cherries, and pineapples. You could see me coming a mile away and that's about how far Russell stayed. He always detested that outfit, calling it (and me) tootie-fruity.

When my two sisters and I were growing up, Mama sewed all our clothes: poodle skirts, shifts, shirt-waist dresses, Madras blouses with Peter-Pan collars, wrap-around skirts, even two-piece bathing suits. She was so creative that she often used one pattern and altered it to make many different styles. She was talented in other ways, too:

she sewed Barbie doll clothes. The latter is truly unfathomable to me. Can you imagine the patience involved with that craft—the intricate measuring and cutting, the resultant sore fingers, crossed eyes, and aching back from sewing those tiny scraps of material? No, thank you!

But here's where Mama's hibiscus capris came into the picture. Getting back to my visit and the morning we were packing to leave, Mama disappeared into her bedroom, getting ready for the day. I'll never forget the sheepish grin on her face when she opened her bedroom door and out she stepped, looking like a million dollars—tah dah!—in living color. I took a double-take. My mama was a fashionista (though I didn't know it at the time because I hadn't read that article yet). Not only was she a fashionista, she was a visionary!

I'd dare anyone to match her beauty that day. Gwyneth Paltrow didn't have a thing over her, unless you consider the fact that Gwyneth is taller. But y'all, my Mama was styling! "If you don't believe it, just ask me!" an old friend used to say.

The rest of that morning Mama was strutting around like a proud peacock, dressed in her turquoise, fuchsia, and yellow hibiscus flowered capris. Her ensemble was complete with a solid turquoise V-neck cotton tee shirt and her comfy Sesto Meucci sandals. Though I lavished praise upon her, I was puzzled. I asked her why she didn't wear that snazzy outfit the day before when we went out to lunch at Chili's (a tradition that I'll explain momentarily). She said, "Because I was afraid this outfit was too loud!" I said, "Mama, that's the point. Loud is good!" She just blushed and said innocently, "Are you sure?" She is so darned cute. I swear the older I get, the younger she looks. Her skin is so smooth and soft, and she has no wrinkles. I mean it. None. I hope her youthful genes have indeed been passed down to me and my family.

I told her the next time we come home, I am going to insist she wears those funky hibiscus capris and blue top when we dine at Chili's. We always have lunch there on Saturday, and now know many of the waitresses by name. Our routine rarely varies: We split an order of fajitas—Mom chooses chicken and I choose steak. When the waitress brings out those steaming hot fajitas in that sizzling cast iron black skillet, I spread out Mom's chicken and cheese on the warm "flour" as Kelly, my oldest daughter, calls it—so it'll melt in a hurry. Then Mom adds the other "fixins" while I prepare mine. I love this dish because I certainly can't duplicate the flavor at home (nor would I want to make that big of a mess) and I'm a huge fan of anything with a charcoaled flavor. Plus the dish (or "presentation," if you will, for all you foodies), is beautiful—almost as colorful as Mama's capris—with the red tomato, green guacamole, and purple onion. Even if it doesn't taste good (just kidding—it always does), it sure looks good. After lunch, we generally visit unique shops not found in my area. During one visit, we even had a pedicure.

Meanwhile, the guys are doing their guy thing. Dad and Russell start their day with a big breakfast at the local country club, then play a round (or two) of golf. Sometimes we find them chair-napping when we make it home later in the day. Then we four regroup, freshen up, and, you guessed it, go out to dinner. What a life, huh?

We're planning another trip to see my parents in a few days and as usual, we'll enjoy these special traditions that I wouldn't trade for anything in the world. But this time, when Mama starts perusing the clothes racks, I'm going to be stuck to her like glue. If I want to make a fashion statement, what better trendsetter to follow?

Who Is Number One
on Your Speed Dialing List?

With everyone staying so busy these days, I've got a little tip that can free up some of your precious time so you can get around to the really important things—like aerating your lawn or hosting a garage sale. This modern convenience that I'm referring to is none other than…speed dialing! Okay, I realize it's not modern. It's been around since, what, the 1970s? But until recently, I never knew what a difference it makes to pick up my cellphone and punch number one for my parents or number two for Kelly, our daughter in Raleigh. Of course, this "convenience" brings up another whole set of problems, like, who is going to be number one on your list? Everyone wants to be, right?

You can choose the order alphabetically, which makes sense. But do you choose the person's last name or first name—and in the case of a couple, do you choose his or her first name? And it's not as simple as choosing one number per family. Oh no! I just realized that my sister Cathy in Virginia Beach, is represented by *ten* separate phone numbers: their home number, their two daughters' home numbers, everyone's cell number, and three out of four have a work number.

Another possibility is prioritizing the speed dialing hierarchy based on where folks live: the farther away, the lower the number. That's pretty simple. In this case, any relatives living in Zimbabwe, for instance, are definitely number one. No argument there.

Another alternative might be to assign the top spot to the person you talk to most often. But then that could cause sibling (or even spousal) rivalry—or at the very least, jealousy. However, under no circumstances do you want to program in your favorite person as number one—that might tick somebody off, or heaven forbid, get you cut out of the family will.

My mother discovered the convenience of speed dialing many years ago. In fact, while I was visiting her recently, she picked up the phone to call Anna (one of her closest friends) to tell her we were leaving to pick her up for dinner. But Mom punched six instead of eight, and she ended up talking to Catherine, another dear friend. Mom felt like a fool, stammering for *something* to say, with only randomness following. She muttered something about the humidity in California (Mom lives in North Carolina), which led to discussing global warming, which led to an opinion of that new movie "The Day After Tomorrow." Quite frankly, it was Weirdsville! Finally, she hung up—probably leaving Catherine worried that Mom had lost her mind.

Mom tried dialing again. Oops! This time she reached Shirley, another buddy. Shirley wasn't home, so Mom got lucky on that one, hanging up without leaving a message. (Even Emily Post doesn't leave a *message* of "Sorry, wrong number"—does she?) Mom then confessed the problem: Without her glasses, she couldn't distinguish the speed dialing number list on her phone. I offered to dial for her, but she refused, protectively cradling that little white phone in her lap.

That was when I got suspicious. I started putting two and two together, so to speak, on the placement of the numbers. I asked her, "By the way, Mom, who's number one on your list?" Do you know she would not tell me! Oh sure, she reiterated the fact that she couldn't read it, so I handed her a pair of reading glasses. Still, no reply. I started getting paranoid, thinking, *What number am I?* Could it be that I'm at the bottom of the list, or worse yet (gasp!), not on the list at all? Eeeyow! Mom gave up on phoning Anna, saying, "Oh, let's just drive over." I'm not sure, but I think I saw her hide the phone.

Speed dialing has helped me in other ways. You know how in some families, one person is designated to keep "the list"? The list includes everyone's home number, cell number, home e-mail address, work e-mail address, Web site, and personal address. Well, in my family that someone just happens to be *me*, and the list is now three full pages long. See, this is where speed dialing could help: the list could be eliminated or at least shortened. No, then some busybody would probably suggest I add our family's social security numbers and blood types to the list. Whew! Things used to be simpler.

Some might even say, "Remember the good old days?" But thinking back, were they really all that good? I'd say not, when you consider party lines and busy signals.

Well, getting back to speed dialing on my cellphone. It's been such a success that I'm finally ready to program speed dialing on my home phone. Who am I kidding? I never programmed the first set of numbers. I left that up to my college daughter, Katie, who is into all this technological hoopla, a "techie," I believe they're called. I am convinced we baby boomers (oh, okay, me anyway) are missing the gene that helps us to understand how CDs, DVDs, MP3s, Palm Pilots, digital cameras, fax machines, scanners, printers, copiers, and speed dial *really* work.

Another advantage to having Katie program the numbers: She can punch them in at random—in no particular order—from one to thirty (or whatever). That way, no one can accuse me of not making them number one in my life (in my speed dialing, anyway). This also assures me that Katie and I will never have that conversation—the one Mom and I had after I came home from visiting her. When I walked in the front door, my phone rung and Mom said, "Cathy? Is that you? Oh, I'm sorry I thought I dialed one." So, *that's* who's number one!

Getting an Education in Grandmotherhood

It wasn't like we didn't have plenty of warning—six months, to be exact. Or that the job was difficult, babysitting our precious granddaughter for the weekend. Or that we knew nothing about children, having raised two daughters of our own. We gladly offered to let Madison stay here while our daughter Kelly and her husband, Chuck, vacationed.

Telling this story to friends, I was met with skepticism. One dubious woman sniffed and said, "Good luck." Another nodded and said, "You're in for a treeeeeeat," but failed to elaborate. I cringed, then thought, *What could go wrong?* Interestingly, one young mother of four daughters said, "My mother has been running a 'Granny Camp' for several summers. Her theory is to 'keep 'em busy, or you'll wind up in a tizzy.'" She offhandedly suggested activities like horseback riding, theatre going, or museum touring. "Do what?" I muttered. "And just remember *to hang loose*," she added. "Hang loose—who, me?" I said, with a furrowed brow.

Well. Madison's attention span was too short for a theatre show or museum tour, and getting her up on a saddle was out of the question! Keeping this in mind, I devised my own Grammy Annie's Camp. This would include cake baking, sandcastle building, reading books, a manicure, blowing bubbles outside, and watching, at Kelly's suggestion, a Wiggles video—a quartet of ridiculously silly Australian boy-men who dress much too brightly and sing strange songs with high-pitched voices. Quite frankly, they scare me and they grate on everyone's nerves except Madison's!

For Madison's visit, my sister Nancy came from Raleigh to offer necessary field support. Our daughter Katie provided much needed back-up support, and Russell himself took over the mission a few times. Indeed, it took four adults to keep up with, as it turned out, this fast-as-lightening, ants-in-her-pants, full-of-herself little squirt.

In fact, my mother calls Madison "the home wrecker" because of a tendency to wreck homes, leaving most things in her path destroyed. Mama also calls her "Little Ann," though I can't imagine why.

I don't believe Madison is so different from other three-year-olds. Still, she is a real study in human evolution. She begans each morning full of energy, excitement, and enthusiasm. "What's that?" shows her curious side. "I can do it myself!" shows her independent side. "I don't want to," shows her stubborn side, and "I love you so much!" shows her loving side. She also has a playful, albeit teasing side, which both delights and exasperates us all.

One afternoon, I let her water my flower and herb garden. When I turned my back for a mere second, she turned the hose on *me*. I promptly took the hose away and watched her dormant "terrible two's" resurface—squeals of delight turned to screams of resistance. Another time, I gave her the empty bowl of cake batter to finish. I poured the batter itself into the cake pan, then walked over to the oven to turn it on. Again, I turned my back for a mere second. Uh oh! Too much temptation. Madison darted to the cake pan and ran all of her fingers through the batter. Thank goodness for Spray 'n Wash because her hands were full of gooey chocolate, and so was her pretty pink blouse.

Once she gave me a big bear hug, saying, "I love you Grammy!" Then she held my face with her tiny hands, eyeing something quite fascinating. Finally she said, "Grammy, you have a pole on your face." A what? I decided she meant a mole. When we were in the mall, she asked me if my watch turned blue. She said her daddy's does and that Katie's does. I was baffled, then realized she was referring to the light-up dial feature. What an education I was getting!

Madison is independent in a way unlike any child I've known. She dresses herself (even socks and shoes, although buckles require help), brushes her teeth, and sleeps alone. But she hasn't mastered potty training. Bribery has helped only to a point: jellybeans, Hershey's Kisses, even lollipops. Initially the candy worked because she's never eaten sugary sweets. Well, that wore off. The bribery stash has now been upgraded to Matchbox cars, if she will just poop in the potty. The other "half" of her training has been accomplished.

Just like her Grammy and her aunts, she loves shopping. One day, I bought her several beach toys and Nancy bought her Dora the Explorer underclothes. At bedtime, Madison opened the package saying, "I'm laying out these new panties in case I have an accident." So we know she understands the concept, but for some reason, she is still holding on—or should I say "holding in"? Hmmm...

Our visit ended today when Madison went home. I sure miss that blue-eyed, sandy blonde three-and-a-half-foot-tall princess running through the house with squeals of laughter. After lunch, I said to Russell, "Geez Louise, suddenly I feel soooooo tired. Think I'll take a little siesta." While I'm normally not one to sleep in the middle of the day, I *craved* a nap. My body went limp, my speech became slurred, and I felt like I was walking in quicksand up to my knees. I trudged along to the bedroom, telling Russell I'd be up shortly, then I literally crawled into bed.

Four *hours* later, I woke up in a fog, thinking, *Where am I? What day is this? Why is everything so quiet?* I stumbled to my feet, washed the sleep from my puffy eyes, and ran a brush through my wild hair. The clock read six o'clock, so I went looking for Russell, whom I just knew was worried about me sleeping that long. Ha! Not a chance. I found him sprawled on the sofa, sawing logs himself. I punched him awake. After freshening up, we went out for dinner. Beside us sat a little girl about Madison's age, with, I guessed, her grandmother. I almost asked, "So how's 'Granny Camp' going?"

Oh No!
Mama Has Become Me

Y ou've heard the old adage, "I've become my mother." I'm afraid the opposite is happening with us, hence: "Mama has become me." On a trip to my parents' home, Mama and I ended up sleeping in the same bed. The end result was, of course, disastrous. Neither of us got much sleep, but I learned a lot in the process.

Let me explain. For years, I've slept with an electric fan blowing. Winter or summer, rain or shine, I have to hear the steady "whir" of the fan to fall asleep. That's my thing: a fan.

Mama's thing, on the other hand, is music. Ever since Dad gave her a Bose Wave CD player a few years back, she goes to sleep with music playing softly (or so I thought) in the background. Normally, she listens to the sounds of Barbra Streisand, Pachelbel, or Allison Krauss (you've got to hand it to her, her taste is eclectic).

How we ended up in the same bed is a story in itself: When I arrived that day, I unloaded my things in the larger of two guest rooms—the number one room, I call it. It's the one with the queen-size bed and the larger closet, as opposed to the number two room with the twin beds and the smaller closet. Russell and I always stay in the number one room, but he didn't come along this time.

When bedtime approached, I told Mama goodnight. She asked me where was I sleeping and I told her. That's when she suggested we sleep together because that was her favorite bed and because she already had her music set up in there. It didn't seem like a big deal, so I said fine.

About an hour later, I was lying there fast asleep when I bolted upright. I heard a lovely but loud operatic voice wafting through the air, accompanied by heavy percussion and…what was that? A wooden flute?

Sarah Brightman was signing "Harem," from her CD of the same name. However, the words sounded more like "welcoming you to my *horror*" instead of "harem." In fact, it felt like horror to me, hearing the thumping and arias going on, well past midnight. I lay there tormented—wide-awake and unable to fall back asleep. Who would have guessed? My seventy-something-year-old mother listening to popular music, and her fifty-something-year-old daughter whining, "Mama, could you please turn that music down?" (Something she regularly fussed about to me when I was a teenager.) I thought, *Oh no! My mother has become me!*

The next morning we discussed our non-quality-of-life sleeping arrangements and the apparent "problems." From my viewpoint, her music kept me awake. From her viewpoint, my fan left her no choice but to play the CD loudly.

We agreed we'd try it again that night, but if problems persisted, I'd move to the number two room. (I realize I was just being lazy, not wanting to move the fan and also not wanting to move all my stuff. My shoe bag alone weighed twenty pounds.)

That night, we got in bed at the same time. I turned on my fan and Mama turned on her CD. Hard as I tried, I could not tune it out. It wasn't so much the singing as it was the frenetic beat and the pounding of the drums. I should've realized with a title like "Harem" the music would be both blaring and distracting. I exhaled loudly—several times, I might add. Mama finally sensed my predicament, got up, and turned off the music, then slipped quietly back into bed. *Oh great.* Then I felt guilty. Instead of the music keeping me awake, the *guilt* took over, keeping me awake.

Finally, peace came…but not for long. I rolled over, and Mama started snoring. Let me ask you something. When was the last time you slept in the same bed with your mama? It's not a good idea!

Here I was with cold feet, hot flashes, and a headache—all compounded with guilt. And it was 1:30 a.m. Weary but stubborn, I remained there.

The next morning, Mama said she fell asleep okay, but woke up often. I asked her was that because her music wasn't playing? She said no, it was because I was snoring! Me? I couldn't believe it! I don't snore. At least, I don't *think* I snore. True, Russell says I "puff" when I sleep, but surely I don't snore. (Do I?)

On the third night of this insufferable insomnia, Mama tried to play "Let's make a deal," saying she'd keep her music off if I'd keep my fan off. *No can do*, I thought. Instead, I prepared to move to the other room, but Mama insisted I stay. We got in bed. The room was quiet. I snuggled down into a comfy position and began dozing off. Ahhhh. Suddenly I heard rattling. "What the—?" I tore off the covers, flipped on the light, and darted towards the noise. It was the fan, of all things—apparently Dad used wire to replace a missing screw and the wire had become loose. With a few choice words, I tightened it and lay back down.

The next night, I was all about room number two. Mama didn't argue. I set up the repaired fan, stretched out on the twin bed (as much as I could stretch), and waited for that one unattainable goal I craved so desperately: a good night's sleep. Sadly, it was not to be. You see, the number two room faces east; and when 6:30 a.m. rolled around, the room lights up like a Christmas tree, blasting out heat and stuffiness.

Midday I found myself groggy and irritable—gee, I wonder why? Exhausted, I crawled to the number one room and lay down. I was half dreaming, when the shrill *rrrrring* of the telephone woke me up. Mama's girlfriend was calling and Mama was giggling like a schoolgirl. I couldn't help but smile, thinking once again that yes, Mama had become me. To witness my mother's happiness was more gratifying than any good night of sleep—and I can always do that when I get home.

Family Follies and Personal Perils

My family seems to have all the luck—bad luck, that is. If there is a nasty hair to be found during dinner, Kelly, our oldest, will be the one to find it on *her* plate. If there is a menacing water bug to be found late at night, Katie, our youngest, will be the one to find it in *her* bedroom. What is it about my daughters that attract bad luck? Oh. I just answered myself. They are *my* daughters, indeed.

Once at a charity golf tournament, Katie and I volunteered to help Russell by watching from a golf cart near the green on a Par three. Our task was to verify any holes-in-one. Not being familiar with the sport, we positioned ourselves too close to the green and were immediately scolded by a ranger to "move away from the whizzing balls flying overhead." And there was that time Katie and I set up our lounge chairs right in the middle of a game of horseshoes on the beach. How were we to know?

One night Russell and Kelly were going out to pick up a meal to-go. Nancy told them to take her car since she was parked in back. Russell heard this, but Kelly didn't. They both sat there a while in separate cars until Kelly looked out from inside our car, parked in the garage, and saw Russell inside Nancy's car, waiting in the driveway. Amazingly, this "ditz-ease/ditziness" has rarely affected Russell—the only level-headed one in the bunch...though there was that time he ended up in the hospital ER with a bleeding tongue from a piece of chewing gum that went awry.

And now that I ponder this phenomenon, I realize even my nephew Huck (Nancy's son) and his fiancée, Heather, aren't immune. They told me about a strange thing that happened when they volunteered at their church nursery: The fire alarm went off right in the middle of the eleven o'clock service. Panicked, Huck and Heather fumbled around, trying to scoop up five squirming babies, aged six to nine months. Dozens of other volunteers and children scrambled about simultaneously, running out of the building en masse. Everyone covered their ears to the sound of the ear-splitting *beeeeeeeep* of the alarm, which droned out any possible communication. Next, the nursery supervisor zoomed past them, urging Huck and Heather to "throw some of the babies in the crib and hold the others."

Following her orders, they put three babies in a crib, then carried one baby each. They then proceeded to a grassy courtyard outside, cradling one baby each, and using their free hand to move the crib with the other babies through the thick green grass. The wheels locked up as Heather and Huck pushed and pulled, going forward, then backwards, then sideways—each of them dizzy, out of breath, and trembling, with an adrenaline rush. Can you imagine what this fiasco looked like from the road? The lawn was packed with a confused congregation, frantic nursery folks, a stunned minister, and one very naughty kid, who they discovered later, had pulled the fire alarm. I'd hate to have that on my conscience for the rest of my life.

Another calamity happened when we were out of town, having dinner with family at a nearby restaurant. My brother, Steve, asked Katie if she'd like to ride back with them. In the parking lot, Katie somehow lost Steve and his wife, Lori, but then caught sight of their green Explorer. She eagerly jumped in the back seat, only to discover Steve and Lori were *not* in the front seat. The stunned driver and passenger never knew what hit 'em, or what left 'em, as the case might be. After all, Katie was with the wrong family.

While the list is long, just in case you're wondering, here are a couple of my more horrific, embarrassing moments: When I was interviewed on TV and didn't realize the cameras were "rolling"; and the first time I ever went on a cruise and thought during the drill that after we donned our life preservers, we *had to jump in the ocean*, just to make sure everything was working. Well, everything wasn't working. My brain is a fine example.

I guess all of this just shows to go you: My family's follies and personal perils have proved a rich, fertile ground in which to write. And thankfully for you all, it's a safe one where no one gets hurt!

Acknowledgements

Thank you to my precious family: Russell and Katie; and Kelly, Chuck, Madison, and Carly Ann Stunda; my parents, Billy and Louise Morris; my sisters, Nancy Huxley and Cathy Smith; and my brother Steve Morris; and their families. A special thanks to Chuck and Carolyn Gee, Ron Osborne, Carol and Eugene Streng, Betty Beamguard, Pam Bell, Madelene Fulcher, Jane Sawyer, Susie Collins, Timi Ray, the late Kimi Blythe, and friends at First United Methodist Church Myrtle Beach. Hats off to Lavin Cars for trusting us with a BMW Z4 (photography prop); Susan Stox of Susan Stox & Co. Salon & Day Spa for hair and make-up; and to Stein Mart for apparel. In gratitude to *Georgetown Times*, *Sasee*, *Myrtle Beach Herald*, *Columbia County Magazine*, *Camden Chronicle Independent*, libraries, bookstores, gift shops, readers, and friends. Finally, a high-five to my superb editor, Emily-Sarah Lineback, and outstanding layout and design artist, Scott Whitaker.